EXPLORING THE ALASKA-YUKON BORDERCOUNTRY

Wrangell-St. Elias National Park
Kluane National Park Reserve
Tetlin National Wildlife Refuge

Text by Jill De La Hunt
Photography and Sidebars by John W. Page

NorthWord
PRESS, INC
Minocqua, WI 54548

ALASKA
NATURAL HISTORY ASSOCIATION

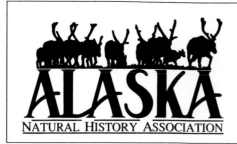

A portion of the proceeds of this book will support the educational programs and services of the Alaska Natural History Association, a nonprofit group dedicated to enhancing the public's understanding of Alaska's natural, cultural, and historical resources. For more information about the association contact:

ANHA, 605 W. 4th Ave., Suite #85, Anchorage, AK 99501

NorthWord Press, Inc.
P.O. Box 1360
Minocqua, WI 54548

Designed by Seth Whynaucht/Wayne C. Parmley
Cover design by Wayne C. Parmley
Project coordinator: Frankie Barker, ANHA
Addtional Photography Copyright © 1994 Stephen J. Krasemann
Pages 15, 37, 69, 70, 80, 92, 94, 107, 108, 112, 114 & 129

Printed and bound in Hong Kong

For a free catalog describing NorthWord's
line of nature books and gifts, call 1-800-336-5666

Library of Congress Cataloguing-in-Publication Data

De la Hunt, Jill.
    Exploring the Alaska-Yukon bordercounty / by Jill De la Hunt :
photography by John W. Page.
       p. cm.
      ISBN 1-55971-430-1 (hardcov) : $29.95. — ISBN 1-55971-438-7
(softcov) : $19.95
       1. Alaska—Pictorial works. 2. Alaska—Description and travel.
3. Wilderness areas—Alaska. 4. National parks and reserves—Alaska.
5. Yukon Territory—Pictorial works. 6. Yukon Territory—Description
and travel. 7. Wilderness areas—Yukon Territory.
I. Page, John W. II. Title.
971.9'1—dc20   94-19315
                                      CIP

Dedications

Together, we are honored to give special acknowledgment to the memory
of Lee Westenburg, former Tetlin National Wildlife Refuge Outdoor
Recreation Planner. Lee had a special love for the Refuge, and was the first
to conceive of a book about the Bordercountry. Lee died at the young age
of 32; his ashes were scattered over the Refuge and are now part of Tetlin
lands and lifecycles. Although Lee did not live to see his idea become
this book, his spirit runs through these pages.

Sue Matthews, Refuge Manager of Tetlin National Wildlife Refuge
Karen Wade, Superintendent of Wrangell-St. Elias National Park and Preserve
Al Fisk, Director of the Yukon–Department of Canadian Heritage

To Mercedes, whose spirit led me North;
To Sylvia, who offered me safe harbor; and
To my parents, who knew I could do it.

Jill De La Hunt

To Mom and Dad, who gave me the
confidence to pursue my dreams.

John W. Page

Acknowledgments

This book is made possible through a joint publishing arrangement with the Alaska Natural History Association, a nonprofit organization dedicated to enhancing the public's understanding and the conservation of Alaska's natural, cultural, and historical resources by working in cooperation with land management agencies and other educational organizations in Alaska.

If you have ever watched a television broadcast of the Academy Awards from Hollywood, California, you probably have wondered why those movie stars ramble on with thanks to people only they know. We have wondered the same thing but now understand. The people with their names in the limelight are only one part of a project. Many people made this book happen, and if we tried to thank them all, you would change the channel. So here is an abbreviated list:

JILL AND JOHN WANT TO THANK:
Frankie Barker, who gets our deepest graditude for more reasons than we will publicly admit to;
The staff at the Alaska Natural History Association, who let us be more than names on an answering machine;
Wenda and Brent Liddle, who showed us that Canadians are wonderful people, even to Americans;
Karen Duchow, friend, sister, and travelling buddy;
The Alaska Division of Tourism for financial support; and finally,
Many thanks to the staff at Kluane National Park Reserve, Tetlin National Wildlife Refuge, and Wrangell-St. Elias National Park for their assistance and support.

JILL GIVES:
Thanks to companion spirits Annie Benson, Jean Bodeau, Karen Button, Laurie Daniel, Mei Mei Evans, Sue Miskell, Moose, and Namche for their boundless love;
Thanks to my brother Mike for letting me call him Dr. Buckwheat;
Thanks to Jim Atwater for hearing my writing voice;
Thanks to Ingrid Seversen and Carol Hoke for their patience and gentleness; and
Thanks to Dave Hik for helping me to see some things for myself.

Table of Contents

Invitation

Greetings! We welcome you to a place we love.

Like many of you, we ventured North for mountain wilds. We came to view glaciers that eons ago polished Canada and the continental United States into rolls of rich farmland. Like many of you, we were in awe of peaks appearing to hold up the sky, rivers roaring cobalt blue through granite canyons, and bear tracks larger than our footprints. We still are. The North is now home.

Alaska and the Yukon hold many powerful places. Some of the most magical spots are in the area we call the Bordercountry: Kluane National Park Reserve, Tetlin National Wildlife Refuge, and Wrangell-St. Elias National Park Reserve. Highest of mountains, longest of glaciers, richest of histories, largest of plant and animal sanctuaries: This is the Bordercountry.

In 1979, the United Nations UNESCO World Heritage Convention recognized Wrangell-St. Elias and Kluane national parks as a joint wilderness site of global importance. The United Nations added Alaska's Glacier Bay National Park, next-door neighbor to Wrangell-St. Elias and Kluane, to the World Heritage list in 1992. The following year British Columbia declared another neighboring site—more than two million acres (nearly nine hundred thousand hectares) of the Tatenshini River drainage—as a provincial park. The combined national and provincial parks comprise over 21 million acres (nearly 8.5 million hectares)—the second largest protected wilderness in the world.

Dictionaries define "border" and "boundary" as designations of fixed limits, as outer confines of space. Bordercountry lines do indeed mark limits because lands outside are more vulnerable to transitory human ideas of "progress" and "development." In a broader sense, however, Bordercountry boundaries are mutable: ever expanding, ever receding. Fixed political borders between Alaska and the Yukon or between public and private lands are meaningless to plants, animals, rocks, rivers, and glaciers. Nonhuman borders change with season, elevation, and age.

Humans use straight-edged maps to determine our location and to decide where to go. Once we realize we are always somewhere, we can put the charts aside. Smell the air, feel the water, listen to the wild. Boundaries exist only where we create them.

These pages and photographs are what we discovered as we tramped the lands and tiptoed through library stacks. We do not know the Bordercountry as professional scientists or anthropologists, nor do we know the land as rooted Athabaskan, Tlingit, Chugach Eskimo, or Eyak native peoples. But we do know the Bordercountry as lovers of place. Our love for this country is what we want to share with you.

For all its rugged beauty, the Bordercountry is vulnerable. This magical place is threatened by logging, mining, and other forms of ecological destruction. Please do all you can to protect the places you visit. Imagine your actions multiplied by ten thousand before you pick a tundra flower or drop a scrap on the ground.

We hope our writings and photographs will help you to come to know the land in your own way. Thank you for reading our book.

Peace and happy journeys.

April 20, 1994
Anchorage, Alaska

Kluane Lake reflections

chapter one

HUMAN PASSAGES:
HISTORY

History. His-story, her-story, their-story, our-story. Whose story? The story is on the tongue of the teller and in the ear of the listener.

History has both Greek and Roman roots. The Greek word signifies an active learning process, a learning of one's story through inquiry. Romans used the term to indicate tales of the past.

Here is a story: Gold miners first came through the Bordercountry in numbers during the Klondike Rush of 1898. Thousands of white men knowing nothing of subpolar wilderness climbed avalanche chutes in minus ten degrees Fahrenheit (minus 23 degrees C) to find riches. Some froze, some starved. Some struck gold, then lost it in the dance halls of Dawson. Most went home within a few years with an abundance of adventures and little else.

Here is another tale: Once, a long time ago, a man climbed the high glaciers of Nay'ayat (now called Mount Natazhat in the St. Elias range). The way was steep, and he cut ice steps with the iron and copper picks he carried. The steps melted behind him; he could find no descending route. Slowly, he became another rock on the mountain. His iron pick fell to the sea, his copper pick to the interior. That is why the interior Bordercountry is veined with copper.

Each event is part of cultural "history." One may be written in a textbook, the other recounted over a cup of tea. Neither is more "true." They are merely different ways to pass on lessons and remembrances of things people believe to be important.

Things people find important depend on their experiences and concepts of self and the world. Are the storytellers women or men? How do they live? Do they cook and tan hides, hunt and trap, or mine copper? Are they officers on a Russian reconnaissance vessel or wives and mothers waiting in Saint Petersburg?

9

Prickley Wild rose

Does survival depend on mastering tracks across white snow or tracks across white paper? Are songs an orientation to place or entertainment? Do marriages connect individuals or clans? How is wealth measured?

And perhaps the most important question of all: Where is home? The mountains, the ocean, the river, the marshlands, Nebraska, or Nova Scotia? Some people have never slept on a groaning glacier; others have never had a meal in a French restaurant. Some feel vulnerable in the Bordercountry and others feel vulnerable in Anchorage. Some look at Devil's Club and appreciate why a botanist named the prickled plant *Echinopanax horridum* ("horrible weapon"); others see a remedy for colds. Different understandings, different stories.

The Bordercountry has many "histories." Histories of rocks, plants, animals, and people. For every history, there is a "historian." Scientists study a history of interdependent life and call it *ecology*, study a story of rock movement and call it *geology*. Athabaskans and Tlingits recount antics of Raven. Christians tell a tale of a six-day creation. Each of us thinks our story is the truth.

But each story is rooted in time, place, and culture. Rooted in experience. What if the historian were a blind man with an acute sense of smell? A young woman sequestered to celebrate her first menses? A man from southern climates feeling cold and snow for the first time? A woman dependent on fall salmon for winter survival?

As you read historical accounts of people traveling over the Bering land bridge ten thousand years ago, of Athabaskan-Tlingit-Russian fur trading, or of the construction of the Alaska Highway, remember that histories are stories. Remember that someone is telling the story. Remember that for each story, there are a hundred others.

Ancient Passages

North America's first people came for dinner and stayed for generations. During the last of the Ice Ages, between fifty thousand and ten thousand years ago, ocean depths were more than three hundred feet (90m) lower than today. Exposed submarine lands created a grassy land bridge called Beringia, which linked present-day Siberia to Alaska and the Yukon. Mammoth, bison, and other giant herbivores grazed on rich Beringia fodder. Hungry hunters followed hungry herbivores.

Beringia's ice-free corridor extended across interior Alaska and the Yukon, just north of present-day Tetlin National Wildlife Refuge. Glaciers may have blocked paths to Alberta, Montana, and points farther south until approximately fifteen thousand years ago, but most anthropologists agree that Bordercountry environs eventually became a well-traveled route to the New World.

Mud volcanos in
Wrangell-St. Elias National Park

As a glacier-free refuge, lands near the Bordercountry were home to ancient peoples eleven thousand years ago. The oldest campsites and tools found in Kluane, Tetlin, and Wrangell-St. Elias to date are between six and eight thousand years old.

Early Bordercountry peoples camped and hunted near the waters and grasslands of the Tanana, Copper, and Shakwak Valleys. Archaeologists have found several eight-thousand-year-old sites near Kluane. Remnants of spear points, fire chars, and giant bison bones tell a tale of a successful hunt, of bison fat crackling in a cooking fire, and of full stomachs.

Ancient people of the North were adaptive nomads. Over time, the large mammals of the Ice Ages disappeared, temperatures warmed, and glacial lakes drained to marsh and grasslands. The people changed with the climate.

Because tools and weapons are the most common find, archaeologists categorize early cultures by changes in artifacts. Rare is the archaeological find, however, that offers more than a tantalizing clue to the past. As nomads, people carried their few possessions from camp to camp. Even when the ancients left tools, environmental conditions destroyed most artifacts. Stone and bone implements have survived the longest. Wood, hide, and bark tools usually disintegrate quickly. Oral languages, stories, and spiritual beliefs last only as long as the people.

For five thousand years, the principal tool and weapon in the Bordercountry was a *microblade*, a sharp-edged thin stone tool approximately 1 1/2 inches long (nearly 4cm). People used the blade as an ancient Swiss Army knife: the all purpose wonder tool. Need a surgical instrument, spearhead, sewing scissors, or sculpting chisel? Grab your microblade.

Approximately forty-five hundred years ago, new technology appeared in the Bordercountry. Microblades went out of style in favor of notched points that could be tied to shafts or handles. Skin scrapers changed shape, and people began to chisel stones into fishnet sinkers.

Did the same people invent new tools? Did a new people travel from Siberia to North America? Was there war or peaceful absorption? Technology is mute. We know change occurred, but nothing of the growing pains that may have accompanied technical innovations.

Fast forward another fifteen hundred years. Once again, the weather turns cold, and growing glaciers block rivers into huge glacial lakes. Animals and people drown and freeze. The climate change forces surviving people to find new hunting grounds, to learn the uses of new plants, and to craft warmer clothing. Imagine midsummer Toronto or Toledo temperatures never warming beyond a slight shiver. Imagine watching your only food sources freezing and dying. How would you survive? These people found a way.

Twice in the next fifteen hundred years, volcanos blasted ash over every square meter of the Bordercountry. Traces of light gray ash are still visible along Alaska Highway roadcuts. Ash blanched waters to a cloudy color, later inspiring names such as "White River."

What would you have thought if you had lived in the Bordercountry in times of volcanic eruptions? Imagine: You are gathering plants when you notice clouds turning black-green. An acrid smell of sulfur insults your nostrils. The midday sky turns dark as winter midnight. Sharp particles rain down, covering everything.

For days the terrifying rain continues. Nothing moves. Each time you breathe, small particles enter your body. Perhaps they are injuring your spirit. Everyone coughs, everyone wheezes. Is the world dying? What have your People done to cause such anger in the sky?

Somehow the ancient ones explained the eruptions to themselves and their children. Somehow they endured.

Passages of the People

From the ancient passages of the First Ones descended the Bordercountry peoples. In their own languages, Athabaskans, Tlingits, Chugach Eskimos, and Eyaks are just "the People." Only after the grand delusions of one Italian did they become "Indians." Only after land-hungry humans from other parts of the globe moved in did they become "Natives."

Most Bordercountry People are Athabaskans, a broad linguistic group reaching from the Kutchin of the Northwest Territories to the Navajo and Apache in the southwestern United States. Athabaskans were and are not monocultured. Groups from diverse geographical territories traditionally spoke different dialects, had distinct cultural mores, and historically were not always friendly with one another.

The vast Bordercountry housed several nations. Most Tlingits, carvers of great totem poles and war canoes, traditionally lived on the edge of coastal Wrangell-St. Elias and the Alsek River drainage. A small number of Chugach Eskimos, related broadly to the peoples of the Bering Sea, also lived near the ocean and on coastal islands. Eyaks—a group of Athabaskans—were another coastal people. Aboriginal peoples still live in traditional areas today.

Tlingits were the holders of greatest material wealth among northern peoples. Surrounded by temperate rainforests, rich fisheries, and benign climates, Tlingit peoples did not live on a harsh environmental edge. With time to carve, accumulate, celebrate, and make war, the Tlingits were a formidable influence on nearby Athabaskans.

Tlingit society is a complex weaving of myth and genealogy: as a Tlingit you have a family, a clan, and are part of a moiety (or general division) of either Raven or Wolf. You have special songs, crests, and animal spirits. You may be a Raven-Beaver, a Wolf-Frog, or someone else. You will receive several names in your lifetime, at least one from a clan elder. You trace your ancestry from your mother's family, and you must marry a member of the opposite moiety. If you are a Raven and fall in love with another Raven, you risk death if you attempt to marry each other.

If you are an eighteenth or nineteenth-century Athabaskan from southwest Yukon or the Copper River drainage, you may have met the Tlingits. They have so many things. You barter copper and furs for their shells and fish oil. As Tlingits begin to market the white man's goods, you exchange stacks of fine furs for guns and steel.

Even if you have not seen the Tlingits for yourself, you know them because long ago your people also became Ravens and Wolves. If you are a daughter and your father has a Tlingit trading partner with a son of the opposite moiety, you may be married to him and go to live in foreign coastal lands. You may never see your family again, but you will have strengthened the bond between your clan and that of your husband. You know all will be well, for you are skilled at sewing and tanning. Your mother would not agree to a marriage to a poor hunter. If your husband should die, you know his brother will become your new husband. You will have another family.

Athabaskan or Tlingit, all great events were marked with *potlatches*, or give-aways. Families amassed furs, blankets tinkling with moose-hoof bells, food, and later, guns, calico, and tobacco to give away at the potlatch. Opposite moieties were invited from far and wide, receiving personal invitations delivered by the young men of the host clan.

Each guest donned his or her crest-decorated dance clothing before entering the host village. The honor of clans depended on offering suitable gifts and on fine singing, dancing, and story-telling. If the potlatch commemorated the death of a family member, the mourning relatives blackened their faces with charcoal and wore burlap sacks.

Unlike modern western cultures, the wisdom of elders was greatly respected among peoples of the Bordercountry. No one knew more about the best places to fish, the best ways to trap, the best tanning methods, and the dangers of the trails. Without the knowledge and experience of the old, life would have been much more difficult. In winter, infirm Athabaskan elders were carried on caribou or moose hides from camp to camp. If starvation forced families to move on, they left as much food as possible with the old ones and returned as soon as hunting or fishing was successful.

Grandchildren learned life lessons from their grandparents in the form of stories. In exchange for cutting the elders' wood and carrying their water, the children heard about Raven, the great trickster, and Beaver, the hard worker. They learned of plants to pick in spring and the way to set a spring trap. Because old people were closer to the spirit world, they had greater powers than the youth. Elders had to be kept happy, for they could cast spells over lazy or impudent young ones.

Lone caribou

15

If you were a young person of the Alsek River valley, you might have learned this tale: Once, a boy laughed at an old man who had gone bald. "You are as bare as the hills on which the gopher plays," the boy taunted. "Hush!" said another elder to the boy. "Someday your hair will be gone, too." The bald old man said nothing but went to Naludi (now called the Lowell Glacier on the Alsek River). The elder sat down, and Naludi crossed the river. A big flood (known as Recent Lake Alsek) filled the valleys and killed all the people except the old man who had scolded the disrespectful boy.

Interior Athabaskan adolescent girls and boys prepared for adult responsibilities. Boys rose early in the morning, plunged into ice-cold glacier streams near camp, and took turns beating one another with willow branches. These exercises toughened the boys' bodies in preparation for the physical hardships of hunting and fighting.

Sports developed agility and skills. A favorite game involved a group of young men pulling a moosehide taut into a trampoline. One boy stood in the middle of the skin, trying to land on his feet each time the others tossed him skyward.

Girls learned to sew, cook, gather, trap, and tan hides from their grandmothers and mothers. As a girl neared puberty, she readied for her first menstruation. Her mother insisted she carry extra clothing with her on forays from camp, for as soon as the girl began to spot blood she was required to stop all movement and wait for someone to find her. She then retired to a special brush hut her male relatives had built for her.

For the next few weeks or months, depending on how long her family could maintain her, she was sequestered. Her people believed the girl was coming into a special power and must be alone to learn how to harness it without harming herself or others.

The adolescent girl wore a distinctive moosehide hood covering her face and body. Traditional hoods were beautiful garments decorated with clinking moose or caribou hooves. A raven feather fluttered from the hood in hopes the girl would always have shiny blue-black hair.

Because her power could harm animal spirits, the adolescent ate only dried meat. Women served her water in a special container made from a porcupine or other animal known for easy birthing, and she drank all cold liquids through the legbone of a swan. Each morning she blew on a handful of swan's down to remind herself to be light on her feet. Feathers tied around all her fingers kept her from breaking the taboo against scratching. Despite her feather-fingers, the girl spent most of her time perfecting sewing skills.

When the prescribed period was over or when her family could no longer afford to be without her help, she returned to the camp in new clothes. She was now a woman, able to marry and bear children.

As has always been true, availability of food and climate conditions affected cultural forms. With ocean riches close at hand, coastal Tlingits led more sedentary lifestyles than Athabaskans of the interior Bordercountry. Interior lands did not offer such easy abundance. People were semi-nomadic and lived in small groups. Fewer than two hundred people inhabited the Copper River valley before white people arrived.

Interior peoples moved with the seasons to follow food supplies, traveling an annual circuit of perhaps 150 square miles (38,850 hectares). In late summer and early fall, all were occupied with salmon fishing. Summer and autumn were also gathering and feasting times, the most abundant seasons of the year.

People in areas without significant salmon runs would travel to more salmon-rich waters to catch winter supplies. Families built intricate fish traps that Southern

A Kluane winter on the Cottonwood Trail

Tutchone people still use today at Klukshu (south of Kluane). Three-sided boxes corral the salmon, and sharpened sticks jutting from trap floors discourage fish from fleeing. Once trapped, salmon are easily gaffed. Other Athabaskan peoples used basket-shaped traps yawning from wide mouths to tunnels too narrow for escape. Traditional fish wheels (ferris-wheel-like fish scoopers) and hand-held dip nets still catch salmon at the confluence of the Copper and Chitina rivers below the McCarthy Road.

Summer and fall, women gathered berries and trapped ground squirrels. Men hunted moose, caribou, sheep, and other animals. Caribou hunting was traditionally a communal effort. Several families met to build fences across valleys known to be caribou migration routes. Women, men, and children piled brush 4-5 feet (1.4 m) high between trees and posts to construct fences stretching 1-3 miles (1.6 to 4.8 km) long. The fences guided caribou toward another fence with snares hung in openings. Caribou caught in the fence snares choked to death or struggled to exhaustion and were easily speared.

As men brought fish and game to camp, women cleaned and prepared salmon, moose, and other animals for drying. Hundreds of fish and animals hung from racks as a bulwark against winter starvation. After drying the meat, people tied the supplies in bundles and moved them to sites near winter camps.

In the coldest and darkest part of the winter, people travelled little and stayed close to lakes for winter ice fishing. Cached food supplies usually were exhausted by February. For several lean months, people depended on ice fishing, deadfall traps, and snares to catch game. If hunger became unrelenting, young men might force a bear from its den and kill it. This was very dangerous, for bear spirits were strong, and the hunters had only spears, arrows, and clubs.

Survival in the Bordercountry required cooperation. "Ownership" signified that a clan or family had first rights in a stream or hunting area, but another's request to use the location was rarely refused. First, clan or moiety ties were broad enough that all were related literally or figuratively and could claim to be family. Second, and perhaps

Bull moose

18

more importantly, all knew that one could not live alone in the North. The only rule was respect: Lands and waters must be cared for because they belonged to future as well as present generations.

Passages of the Seekers

Tlingits feasted and carved, Athabaskans fished and hunted, and people traded copper, moose hides, seaweed, and shells. Clans intermarried. Babies were born, elders passed on. Life moved in seasonal cycles.

And change sailed over the horizon. Peter the Great of Russia sent Vitus Bering to claim Alaska as Peter's own.

Dall sheep in Wrangell-St. Elias National Park

In 1741, after ten years of planning, provisioning, transporting, and building, two Russian ships left the Kamchatka Siberian Peninsula in search of America. Storms separated the *Saint Peter* from the *Saint Paul*, and after a few days' search, Captain Bering steered the Saint Peter on a solo journey toward North America.

Historical recountings of Bering's glimpse of Alaska on the Russian Orthodox feast day of Saint Elias are romantic. Picture a long voyage to a land many doubted even existed. Sailors, Cossack servants, young boys learning a trade: sick with scurvy, sipping the last of stored drinking water, weighted with a dread of never returning home. The *Saint Peter* was surrounded by swirls of thick fog, tossed on gray waters. Suddenly, the mists parted to reveal a sunlit crystal peak stretching high as the heavens. All were jubilant. The mountain and lands must be named for patron Saint Elias.

History is woven from fact and fiction. Contemporary narratives from ship physician, scientist, and minister Georg Wilhelm Steller tell a different tale of the Russian "discovery" of Alaska. Bering, greatly concerned with premonitions of death (correct, as it turned out), appeared uninterested in the coastline. As fellow shipmates surrounded the captain to congratulate him on his certain acclaim, Bering "not only reacted indifferently and without particular pleasure but in our very midst shrugged his shoulders while gazing at the land."[1]

Anxious to secure a supply of fresh drinking water and turn homeward, Bering was not inclined to grant Steller long shore leave to explore the natural

[1] *Steller, Georg Wilhelm, Journal of a Voyage with Bering 1741-42 (trans. M. Engel & O. Frost)(Stanford University Press 1988) p. 61.*

Hubbard Glacier separating Russell Fjord from Disenchantment Bay

wonders of America. Within a few hours of landing with the shore party, Steller had found a human habitation and seen a campfire from a distance. But when the scientist sent Bering a report of his finds and a request for more men and time, Bering's "gracious and patriotic answer" was that Steller "'was to get [his] butt on board pronto,' or without waiting, they would leave [him] behind."[1] A frustrated Steller exclaimed, "We have come only to take American water to Asia."[2]

English, French, and Spanish explorers followed on Bering's keel. Unlike most of the Russians, west European adventurers saw Alaska as a side trip secondary to their quests for the mythical Northwest Passage from Europe to the riches of Asia. British Captain James Cook sailed past Yakutat Bay in 1778. French geographer J.F. de Galaup La Perouse saw Mount St. Elias in June of 1786. Spanish Northwest Passage seeker Alejandro Malaspina expressed his frustration in sailing up a dead-end fjord in 1791 by naming the waters "Disenchantment Bay." Finally, in 1794, British captain George Vancouver concluded after extensive shoreline searches that the Northwest Passage did not exist.

[1] *Ibid. at 71.*
[2] *Ibid. at 64.*

Not all Europeans confined probings to the coast. Nor did all explorers gain historical fame. Russian Dmitriv Tarkhanov may have been the first European to travel inland from the Gulf of Alaska. Lord Baranov, governor of Russian-America, believed an interior expedition might reveal either mineral riches or access to the Northwest Passage. After securing permission from Copper River Athabaskans to cross their country, Baranov gave orders to Tarkhanov to travel up the Copper River.

In late fall of 1796, Tarkhanov strapped snowshoes to his boots and tramped inland. He traveled hundreds of frozen miles from Yakutat to the Copper River and up the waterway. Running out of food, Tarkhanov was forced to abandon his journey and return to the coast. Tarkhanov's great adventure is now but an obscure reference in scholarly research indexes.

Between the late eighteenth and early nineteenth centuries, Russian hunters and enslaved Aleut natives hunted the sea otter to near-extinction. In addition, a bloody Tlingit rebellion at the Russian Yakutat fort quelched Russian enthusiasm for coastal posts. Fur-hungry eyes turned inland toward beaver, lynx, wolf, and other interior furbearers. Russians travelled up the Copper drainage and attempted trading near the Athabaskan communities of Taral and Batzulnetas.

Relations between Athabaskans and Russians were strained, and violence occasionally broke out. The cultural pressure cooker finally exploded at Batzulnetas in 1848. The story of Batzulnetas is part of Upper Tanana Athabaskan oral history tapestries. Elders Katie John and Fred John, Sr., recounted the tale in 1973:

> *When the first Russians came up the Copper River and up this way they were mean, they were hungry for blood. Those Russians were probably after fur or something like that. At every village they ask who the chief is and kick him and whip him with a whip with knots on the end. They took everything from the Indians. The Russians come up Slana River to Bazulnetas. The story start in Batzulnetas.*
>
> *Batzulnetas was a big village and had many places. But the Russians took the women and chased out the men from their homes. The Russians killed the dogs and made the women tan the hides. This was something they had never done before. The women had never tanned one dog hide. They took everything: the spears, stick guns (bows), arrows, and all those things the Russians took away. They try to make the Indians starve to death. However, out in the woods the Indians have cache and everything. They just go to the cache and eat the stuff there.*

*They start training for war. We get there and start training our-
selves for war. . . . After they were training three months they send
down some boys to Batzulnetas to tell the women, all the Indian
women, to pack up the Russians' guns with sticks and to put water in
their muzzle loaders. And all the women did that. A lot of Aleuts
came up with the Russians and all those Aleuts understood the language. This Indian chief came up and told them it's going to start
early in the morning; they are going to attack the Russians in the village. And they tell the Aleuts when we start, just sit still. The
Batzulnetas chief talk to the Aleut chief and said we clean that building out at night time by the morning. Don't sleep; get up at midnight.
All the Russians will be sleeping in the building. And the Aleut chief
told his men to sit still.*

*Early in the morning the people in Batzulnetas heard all kinds
of animal noises. That's what they used to do when war, make all
kinds of animal noises. And the village people started to get excited.
They attack. The Russians get up and try to shoot their muzzle loaders but nothing fires. . . . The Indians cleaned everyone out. All the
Russians.*

*The Aleut boys they were all safe and all the Indian women. The
Russians killed only one Native. At the end a big building full of
Russians was ankle deep in blood. They burned up that building;
when I was a child I saw the place where they burned the bodies in
Batzulnetas. That building was full of Russians.*[1]

The Batzulnetas battle ended official Russian presence in interior Alaska.
Twenty years later, the United States purchased "Seward's Folly" from Russia for $7
million. The sovereign native peoples of Alaska were not party to the purchase
agreement.

Farther south, Tlingits refused safe passage and guiding aid to Russians and
other white traders wanting to travel over the coastal Chilkat and Chilkoot passes.
Instead, the Tlingits acted as intermediaries between European fur buyers and
Kluane area Athabaskan hunters. Tlingits conducted trade with Athabaskans at the
village of Nesketahin in the Yukon and with Europeans in coastal Tlingit villages.
Secure in a monopoly, the Tlingits profited from exchanges with both hunters and
buyers.

Scientist George Davidson visited Tlingit Chilkat Chief and Wolf Clan
leader Kohklux of Klukwan on the Stikine River in 1869. Kohklux was an impos-

---

[1] *John, Katie & John Sr., Fred, as told to B. Stephen Strong, "The Killing of the Russians at Batzulnetas
Village," Alaska Journal, Summer 1973 (3/3) pp. 147-48, quoted in Hunt, Wm. R., Mountain
Wilderness: Historic Resource Study for Wrangell-St. Elias National Park & Preserve (National Park
Service, Alaska Region) (Wash., D.C.: Government Printing Office 1991).*

ing warrior over six feet (2 m) tall, who sported a bullet hole in his cheek. Kohklux had a formidable warrior past, including leadership of an 1852 raid to attack an English post in central Yukon. Kohklux and his warriors burned the trading post as a message to Europeans that the Tlingits would protect their lucrative fur-trading monopoly.

Kohklux, however, was the perfect host to Davidson. The scientist was, after all, not interested in furs. He had come to witness a solar eclipse from the vantage point of Klukwan. Henry Seward, then U.S. Secretary of State, joined Davidson for the event.

Kokhlux was impressed with Davidson's foreknowledge of the eclipse and offered to share information about the interior with the scientist. For three days Kokhlux and his two wives drew maps of interior rivers, camps, landmarks, and routes. When compared with modern cartography, Kohklux's map of 1869 is remarkably accurate. Kohklux had the indelible memory of place one gains in tracing lands footfall by footfall.

Davidson recognized the honor Kokhlux bestowed on him. He knew the Chilkats had been reluctant to share knowledge with any stranger, and here was

24

Kokhlux laughing and gesturing that he needed more paper to complete the charts. Perhaps out of esteem for the Chief and his gift, Davidson refrained from publishing Kokhlux's map for another thirty years.

The combination of fierce Tlinglit warriors and daunting terrain kept all but a handful from penetrating the Alaskan interior until the mid-nineteenth century. Most North Americans are familiar with the explorations of Lewis and Clark across the western United States. But how many know of the epic journey of Allen and Fickett?

In 1885, Lieutenant Henry Allen led a small military reconnaissance team, including Private Fred Fickett, over 1,500 miles (2,500km) of Alaskan wilds in five months. Their mission was to assess the value of the newly acquired federal lands and the potential dangers from hostile Native peoples. The Allen party travelled up the Copper River, overland to the Tanana River, up the Tanana to the Yukon River, then down the Yukon to the Koyukuk, and out to the village of Saint Michael on the Bering Sea.

Allen recorded his impressions in personal, geographical, and geological logs. Fickett also kept a journal, but did not have Allen's educated polish. Despite differences, necessity bonded the gentleman officer and the rough scrapper over the length of the arduous journey.

Allen attempted to photograph the expedition. Unfortunately for Allen and history, compact 35-millimeter cameras were not available. Allen and Fickett lugged a heavy tripod box camera and a stack of foot-wide glass photography plates for many miles, but the strains of travel forced the trekkers to lighten their loads. Camera plates were among the first items discarded. Few of Allen's Bordercountry photographs survived.

Starvation was a constant companion on Allen's expedition. A month into the journey, the explorers met an Athabaskan who gave them meat salvaged from a winter wolf kill. Fickett's journal describes their meal:

> *[The Copper River people] had left a few scraps lying round,*
> *and these, that neither they nor their dogs would eat, we were forced*
> *by hunger to gather up and make a meal on. This is Lieutenant Allen's*
> *birthday, and he celebrated it by eating rotten moose meat.*[1]

Allen probably would have died near the Copper River if not for the aid of renowned Chief Nicolai of Taral and other native people. Nicolai was known by native and white peoples as a strong leader with great copper wealth. When the starving Allen party found Nicolai's camp, the chief feted the men with a gargantuan meal of meat and fat. Nicolai then revealed the location of his copper lode to Allen. Ever the efficient information gatherer, Allen noted the site in his report.

[1] *Quoted in Allen, Lieutenant Henry T., An Expedition to The Copper, Tanana, and Koyukuk Rivers in 1885 (Alaska Northwest Pub. Co. Anchorage: 1985) p. 45.*

Allen's logs led to the "discovery" of the Kennecott Copper Mines. Nicolai also provided guides, a boat, and secured food for Allen's journey.

Nicolai's services to the strangers were not free. Once his stomach was full and his strength restored, Allen revealed great irritation at Nicolai's business sense:

> The assistance rendered us by the many natives recently with us was valuable, but their ceremonies and great sense of rank were very oppressive to my party. . . . None of the natives would sell us food of any kind without consulting [Nicolai], and he advised prices that would make a commissary in civilization shudder. They realized full well our dependence, and made the most of it. Instead of acceding to our terms, we were almost invariably compelled to yield to theirs.[1]

Allen's Alaska writings rarely reveal what must have been kaleidoscopic combinations of excitement, discouragement, fear, and awe. The men struggled for weeks to reach the headwaters of the Copper River. When they finally confirmed the river's source, they also realized they were but a few miles from the beginning of the Nabesna/Tanana River, which flows 1,000 miles (1,600km) northwest to the Bering Sea. Although fully aware of the significance of his find, Allen laconically described the discovery as merely "interesting."[2]

Occasionally Allen the Adventurer's exhilaration prevailed over Allen the Soldier-Scientist's detached observation. His words recording the exhausted party's first sight of the Tanana Valley sing:

> On this pass, with both white and yellow buttercups around me and snow within a few feet, I sat proud of the grand sight which no visitor save an Atnatana or Tananatana had ever seen. Fatigue and hunger were for the time forgotten in the great joy at finding our greatest obstacles overcome.[3]

Allen's 1885 maps of the Copper and Tanana Valleys were the only accurate charts available for another three decades and guided many toward the goldfields of the Klondike. Nonetheless, neither Allen, Fickett, nor any other member of the party received any special commendation for their Alaska achievements. As an elderly retired Army officer, Allen wrote several letters on his own behalf, urging Congress to recognize him with a medal and pension. The United States government, however, was no longer interested in Allen and his dusty memories.

[1] Ibid. at 55.
[2] Ibid. at 60.
[3] Ibid. at 62.

Silver City cabin on Kluane Lake

Parallel Passages

European goods affected Interior native lifestyles and cultures long before most Bordercountry people actually saw white men. Interior peoples traded with coastal Tlingits, who had bartering relationships with Europeans. Furs bought guns, steel, and calico materials.

Guns transformed traditional hunting practices by minimizing the need for cooperative efforts. Men began to allocate less time to hunting for food and more time to trapping for trade. Cooking in iron pots saved women hours of labor previously spent heating rocks to boil water in bark containers. But because the men were away trapping for white traders, women depended on the extra time to do chores men had done in the past. Women discarded traditional tanning methods in favor of methods preferred by European skin buyers. Families could no longer afford to be without any set of hands to prepare for winter, so girls shortened their first menstruation ceremonies. Elder women today say the demise of the young women's ceremony greatly contributed to a loss of cultural powers.

Slowly, Bordercountry people began to "need" the white man's material goods. Slowly, imperceptibly at first, cultures transformed one another. Native and white passages assumed parallel paths.

Between the late nineteenth century and the present, sharp points of frenzied activity have punctuated traditional Bordercountry quiescence. Gold rushes, then quiet. Copper mining, then quiet. World War II highway building, then quiet. Oil drilling, tourism, National Parks and Refuges . . . then quiet?

In 1890, a journalist and an adventurer teamed up to cross the Chilkat Pass and bring the first horses to the interior. Edward Glave and Jack Dalton embarked on a challenging trip into the unknown, for they could persuade neither coastal Tlingits nor interior Athabaskans to guide them for most of their journey. Prescient Chilkats had sent word that the men would steal native lands.

Glave knew that without Jack Dalton's wilderness and orienteering genius, the trek would not have happened. Glave may be the antihero of tough bush-whacking legends, for he freely admitted his fondness for the comforts of home:

> *"Roughing it" in the true sense of the expression, is a most cheerless undertaking, to my mind, commendable only as a necessity. During nine years of travel in wild and unfrequented places, my lodgings and board have been strangely varied; but when I can, I like to have a comfortable room and to summon my breakfast by electric button.*[1]

Many of us may see ourselves reflected in Glave's alternate attraction for adventure and distaste for discomfort.

Self-confessed tenderfoot though he may have been, Glave obviously enjoyed a challenge. Not only did Dalton and Glave eventually reach inland, they proved that packhorses could stand the rigors of the journey. The possibilities were lost on neither Glave nor Dalton. Glave gushed:

> *Our successful experiment wrests from the Chilkat Indians the control of the road to the interior; the bolted gate hitherto guarded by them, to the exclusion of enterprise and progress, has swung back at the approach of the packhorse.*[2]

Unlike Glave, Jack Dalton was not a man for flowery prose. But Dalton knew an opportunity when he saw one. In 1894 he established a post near Neskatahin and eliminated middlemen Tlingits from his trading with Athabaskan

[1] *Glave, E.J., Pioneer Packhorses in Alaska: Part II. The Return to the Coast* p. 874.
[2] *ibid., Part I: The Coast* p. 682.

fur trappers. Over the next few years, Dalton widened the Chilkat trading trail and built shelter cabins. He was perfectly positioned to profit from the Klondike Rush without ever lifting a gold pan.

GOLD! The word whispered through the Yukon for many years and grew to a deafening roar by 1897. Would-be millionaires from near and far came North, hoping to find relief from a global economic depression. Most arrived between 1897 and 1898, crossed the Chilkoot or Chilkat passes, paid Jack Dalton $2.50 a head to use "his" trail, and travelled past the Bordercountry to the Klondike. Another six thousand patriotic Americans chose the longer "all-American route" from Valdez to Copper Center, Alaska, then over the Mentasta Pass and on to the Klondike.

Skookum Jim, a Yukon Athabaskan from Tagish, brought on the big strike when he found gold during a moose hunt. Elder Kitty Smith told the story in 1990:

> They hunt now. Nighttime, they came back. It's dark, too, they said. Skookum Jim, he's got a light—a candle. He got a can, put it in—that's the kind they've got. Dawson Charlie, he shot a bull moose, so they cook meat—big eat! They fall asleep—they eat too much!
>
> Skookum Jim wakes up: Carmack is sleeping, Dawson Charlie too. Patsy too. He wants a drink of water . . . He tells me this, you know . . . He's got hat; he wants to drink with that one. The teapot is full of tea. That's why he goes down, puts his hat in the river that way. He see something up there . . . "Is that copper?" He drinks water, looks again. Same big as beans, you know—bigger than beans . . . heavy.
>
> He takes off. He doesn't know gold much, Skookum Jim. Nobody knows gold much. But George, he knows! He goes back. Dawson Charlie wakes up. "I found something," Jim tells him, Indian way. "Don't know what is that. What does it look like?"
>
> "Copper," he [Charlie] says.
>
> "Make George wake up now—it doesn't look like copper. Heavy, too." George wakes up.
>
> "You wake up good?"
>
> "Yeah."
>
> "What is that, this one? That creek I found it."
>
> "That's gold!" Where's their sleep now? That tea is still there. They don't drink much, though! "You see now gold!" George tells them—runs down to creek.[1]

[1] Smith, Kitty as told to Julie Cruikshank, in Cruikshank, J., *Life Lived Like a Story: Life Stories of Three Yukon Native Elders By Julie Cruikshank in collaboration with Angela Sidney, Kitty Smith & Annie Ned* (Univ. of Nebraska Press, Lincoln: 1990) p. 188.

Mountain alpenglow in
Kluane National Park Reserve

Skookum Jim's find changed lives and lands. In a short time, the quiet rhythm of the Bordercountry went BOOM! Miners veered off the Klondike path and into the Bordercountry, following two decades of strike rumors from Bullion Creek and Silver City near Kluane to Chisana in Wrangell-St. Elias.

For Bordercountry native peoples, the boom brought more than European luxuries and guiding jobs. The gold rush meant disease and further cultural disintegration. Many left traditional land-based lifestyles for cash employment. Many died from exposure to diseases new to Athabaskan and Tlingit immune systems.

Thousands of international travelers also reminded the Canadian and U.S. governments that northern borders were not clearly settled. For native peoples, new political borders acted as barriers. The boundary between British Columbia and the Yukon Territory, established in 1895, limited access to traditional southern Athabaskan hunting grounds. Almost all of the village of Neskatahin, 14 miles (22 km) from the new border, moved north to Jack Dalton's new post near Champagne.

When the golden luck ran out, so did most of the white miners. Today, fire-weed weaves through knotholes of remnant Silver City post office walls. Chisana, now home to but a handful, had more log cabins than Fairbanks in 1913. Quintessentially human, some are ever hopeful: Active mining sites still dot the Bordercountry.

A few Europeans felt the call of the Bordercountry and found a way to stay. The French Jacquot Brothers of Burwash Landing on the northwest shore of Kluane Lake started a trophy-hunting business. Moosesteak and wild blueberry flapjack breakfasts were standard Jacquot service. And among the clientele paying to participate in these catered killings were U.S. Senators.

As the gold dust dimmed, miners began to notice the sheen of copper. Native peoples had traded copper for hundreds of years before Chief Nicolai showed his treasure to Henry Allen. But by the first decade of the twentieth century, New York moguls were involved in the copper search. By 1911, the eastern United States fortunes of Guggenheim and Morgan had financed the building of a 120-mile (193-km) railroad: a line blasted, hammered, and torn through the Copper and Chitina River valleys to Kennecott.

At its peak, the Kennecott mines wound in mazes over, under, and around the mountains surrounding McCarthy. Between 1906 and 1930, the mines produced approximately 200 million pounds (90.7 million km) of copper, more than any other mine in North American history.

But what about the people? What was Kennecott to them? For turn-of-the-century immigrants, Kennecott was a paycheck and sixteen-hour shifts in stale, dark tunnels. For children of mining supervisors, the mining town was a northern playground complete with Christmas pageants, ice cream cones made from glacier ice, and picnics in the hills. Today, children and adults find a historical wonder. Kennecott is a museum of early twentieth-century American ideals.

Nature lovers who come to the Bordercountry face a perplexing ethical dilemma: The complete lack of regard for ecological values reflected in old mining trails is shameful, but the roads sure beat hours of alder tussles. Who wants to bushwack when old mining roads wind everywhere? Perhaps the only answer is to use the roads but minimize your own impact on the land.

Not all newcomers sought the Bordercountry for material wealth. Some came to engage the mountains on Nature's terms. American geologist Israel Russell attempted twice to climb 18,008 foot (5,489 m) Mount St. Elias. Tormented by weather, he failed on both trips but established the route to the top.

His Royal Highness Prince Luigi Amedeo di Savoia, Duke of Abruzzi, followed Russell's route and was the first to summit Mount St. Elias. The Count, obviously a companion spirit to Edward Glave, carried folding iron bedstands, condensed cream, salmon, and beef tongue across the Malaspina glacier and up the mountain. Perhaps we should say his nine porters carried these items. The porters declined Abruzzi's offer of iron bedstands for all and hauled only those of the gentlemen climbers.

As the Italian mountain guides neared the summit, they allowed Abruzzi to pass:

> *H.R.H. stepped forward, and was the first to plant his foot on the summit. We hastened breathlessly to join in his triumphant hurrah!*
>
> *Every trace of fatigue disappeared in the joy of success. This moment was the reward of our thirty-eight days of labour and hardship.*[1]

Whatever snickers may come from late twentieth-century climbers who cut toothbrushes in half to eliminate weight, Abruzzi did summit. Without airplane support.

Many early climbs became stories worth telling. Dora Keen, a Bryn Mawr graduate and proper young lady, was the first to summit 16,390-foot (5,466-m) Mount Blackburn in 1912. Climbing in woolen skirts, Keen explained:

> *That I was only five feet [one and a half meters] tall would matter very little. Success would depend rather upon judgment, endurance, courage, and organization. . . . I was going because I had need of courage and inspiration and because on the high mountains I find them as no where else.*[2]

Other mountaineers came to the Bordercountry as surveyors. Their task was to transpose smoke-filled-room diplomacy into real lines over real mountains, valleys, rivers, and muskeg. Neither the political wranglings nor the border measurements were simple tasks.

Look at a map. Does anything appear unusual about the Alaska-Yukon border? Straight as a North Dakota highway from the Arctic Ocean to the St. Elias Range, then jagged as bear teeth across the mountains and down the Alaska Panhandle to British Columbia. See it? No water access. The political line bars the Yukon from the ocean.

Turn-of-the-century U.S. politicos acquiring strategic territories had little interest in watersheds, ecosystems, or the sovereign desires of others. Canadian

[1] De Filippi, Filippo, _The Ascent of Mount St. Elias, Alaska_ (Archibald Constable and Co. London: 1900) pp. 154-55.

[2] Keen, Dora, _First Up Mount Blackburn_, "The World's Work," Nov. 1913, reprinted in Alaska Geographic, _Wrangel-St. Elias: International Mountain Wilderness_ Vol. 8 No. 1 (Anchorage: 1981) pp. 110-111.

children learn a piece of history that many American schoolbooks omit: Nations almost went to war over the location of the line dividing Alaska and the Yukon. In the end, U.S. President Teddy Roosevelt shook his proverbial "big stick" and won the Alaska Panhandle. Canada, who had depended on England to represent its interests, formed its own diplomatic corps after the Alaska border fiasco.

Despite resentments over boundary politics, Canada and the U.S. worked together to mark border lines. American and Canadian surveyors measured a straight line from the Arctic coast to the St. Elias Range. Even more astonishing, between 1904 and 1920, mountaineer surveyors triangulated lines across the peaks of the St. Elias Range to within one foot (one-third meter) of today's computerized calculations. Anonymous and forgotten, the border surveyors were both explorers and adventurers.

Construction of the Alaska Highway is another Bordercountry saga. During World War II, Americans and Canadians were concerned that Japan might try to invade North America through Alaska. Those fears became the 1,600-mile (2,600-km) Alaska-Canada Highway. Yukon Athabaskan guides helped plan the route. Following Tlingit-Athabaskan trading routes, the Al-Can Highway tarred over tradition to bring the future to the North.

The entire military highway was built in nine months. In nine short months, U.S. Army personnel blasted, shoveled, and slogged through the North. Mosquitos bit in the summer, and winds bit in the winter. Army personnel, many of whom were African-Americans segregated from white units in Europe and the Pacific, dug the Alaska-Canada Highway from rock walls, soggy tundra, and ice-cold rivers. In nine months, World War II birthed a twentieth century Bordercountry.

The Alaska-Canada Highway brought further change to Bordercountry native cultures. Unwitting soldiers carried deadly diseases, creating epidemics among Athabaskan peoples. Many died. Those that survived were forced to again call on their ability to adapt.

As you travel through Kluane, Tetlin, and Wrangell-St. Elias, think of the countless footprints under the Alaska Highway. Remember how many threads form Bordercountry story patterns. Then add your own story.

National Park Rangers Jeff Lauersdorf and Jennifer West knew that their stakeout was going to pay off when the hunter appeared carrying Dall sheep horns and a hide, called a cape. For two days the Wrangell-St. Elias seasonal rangers had been monitoring the area around Big Mountain Lake and watching for poachers.

Poaching is a major problem for Wrangell-St. Elias and Kluane national parks. The area is home to trophy-sized Dall sheep. Before establishment of the parks, many of the world's largest Dall sheep were shot in the Wrangell-St. Elias mountains. Most sheep are taken legally. Subsistence hunters can hunt within the Wrangell-St. Elias Park and Preserve, whereas sport hunting is allowed only in the preserve. At Kluane National Park Reserve, hunting is restricted to members of the Southern Tutchone First Nation, who have traditionally hunted in the area.

Poaching occurs when game is taken out of season without permits, when sport hunters hunt within park boundaries, or when subsistence hunters use illegal means to gain access to the park. Subsistence hunters are not allowed to enter the Wrangell-St. Elias Park by aircraft. Restrictions also exist for same-day flying and sport hunting within the preserve. You have to wait until the following morning to hunt.

Wolf, moose, and caribou are occasionally poached. Park officials suspect that a few bears may have been poached for gallbladders, claws, and teeth. Bear gallbladders are used as a medicine in Asia. Most poaching occurs with sheep. Sheep hunting is big business. Average costs for a legal, guided hunt within the Wrangell-St. Elias Preserve is $8,000. When spending this kind of money, most hunters want to get a trophy ram.

Trophy rams are getting harder to find. Large rams appear to be underrepresented within the preserve, probably due to hunting. Biologists question whether the hunting bias for large rams may be reducing genetic diversity by eliminating the larger rams from the breeding stock. To find trophy sheep, some sport hunters step over the line from preserve to park land. Park rangers have cause to believe that a sophisticated poaching network exists. For a fee ranging from $25,000 to over $50,000, the illegal guides provide access and guide service in the park. Using souped-up airplanes, the poachers deliver the client to the area where they had previously spotted big rams.

Dall sheep ram

To avoid detection by the authorities, multiple planes are often used, one serving as a decoy. Camouflaged tents, camping gear, and clothing keep the poachers hidden from view. Secret radio codes keep radio transmissions obscure. With only four field rangers in the 13,000,000-acre (5,260,930 hectare) Wrangell-St. Elias Park, poachers have the advantage. Despite this, each year the Park Service catches a few poachers.

On this day luck was with rangers Lauersdorf and West, who watched as the hunter returned to the small landing strip near Big Mountain Lake. After setting up and camouflaging his tent, the man removed and hid a set of full curl sheep horns and the sheep cape. Summoning the park's helicopter, the rangers made the arrest.

The hunter was found guilty in both federal and state courts of wasting a Dall sheep, unlawfully taking wildlife, and transporting unlawfully taken wildlife. He received fines totaling $3,500, forfeiture of his rifle and spotting scope, loss of hunting privileges for five years, and seven days in jail.

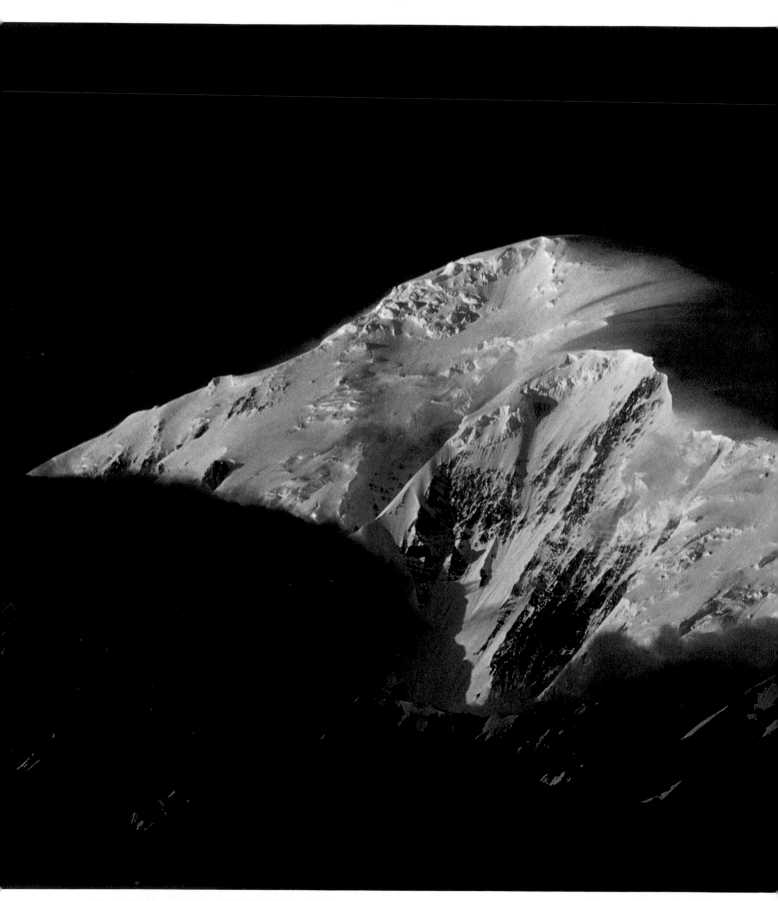

Mount Blackburn in Wrangell-St. Elias National Park

chapter two

EARTH TIME:
GEOLOGY

"**To see** the world in a grain of sand," said poet William Blake, is to "hold infinity in the palm of your hand." Blake may not be known as a geologist, but he summed up the science and art of geology in a neat phrase. That irritating pebble caught in your sock has a story to tell involving oceans, glaciers, mountains, and rivers. That pebble has a story to tell about time and ceaseless change.

Look around. Perhaps you see the Kluane Range stretch above as you drive the Alaska-Canada Highway or vegetation-covered sand dunes across from the Tetlin National Wildlife Refuge. Then again, you may be watching alpenglow tint the massive volcanos of the Wrangell Mountains.

Wherever you are, the land looks timeless, changeless. Do not be deceived. Mountains are on the move. You may not be able to see the motion in a day, a year, or a lifetime, but the clues are there. The pebble in your sock is a clue.

Earth is four and a half billion years old; changes in earth time happen over tens of millions of years. But we are bombarded with large numbers every day. What do they really mean? To comprehend the vast time periods involved in geological change, we have to slow down.

Time lapse films—the kind nature programs use to capture a butterfly emerging wet-winged from a cocoon—may help us see earth time. A camera in place two hundred million years ago could have recorded the lands of the Tetlin Refuge anchoring to North America.

Roll the film to watch slivers of ocean crust and continental lands dock against the North American continent and edge their way north over the next 175 million years to form Wrangell-St. Elias and Kluane parks. Climates changed from cool to warm to cold. Volcanos formed and eroded, glaciers carved, peaks rose. Marine animal skeletons drifted to the bottom of the sea and rode to the top of mountains. This is the rhythm of earth time.

Plate Tectonics

It is Sunday morning. You are making a three-egg omelette. You have cracked two eggs into a bowl and are cracking the third when the telephone rings. Your hand slips and cracked egg shell falls into the bowl. Shell floats on the yolk mixture in tiny jagged pieces. Believe it or not, you are now looking at a model of the earth.

Unbeknown to most of us, a scientific revolution as significant as Darwin's theory of evolution has occurred in the last thirty years. The revolution is the concept of plate tectonics. Plate tectonics explains volcanos, earthquakes, and formation of the Bordercountry. Plate tectonics has made an eggshell of the earth and a crazy quilt of Alaska and the Yukon.

To understand how pieces of the planet can float like eggshells on yolk, we have to know something about earth's innards. Earth is a neapolitan layering of crust, mantle, and core. The rigid outer layer of crust corresponds to the eggshells in our model. The upper mantle under the crust flows like cracked egg yolks. Below, the lower mantle is hotter and more solid. The core is divided into a solid outer thickness and a liquid center.

Earth's crust is broken into six major plates and several smaller ones. Plates do not correspond directly with continents: Some plates are composed solely of ocean bottom, some only of continental lands, and some are a composite of both. As scientists currently understand earth movement, plates interact in three ways. They collide, spread apart, or grind along one another. Movement in the Bordercountry is of the grinding and colliding sort.

Geologists still do not understand the mechanism driving movement of the plates, but many theorize that the answer lies in convection currents powered by radioactive decay. Moving plates engage in the serious work of creation and destruction.

Hot magma oozes through large cracks in ocean floor spreading zones to add new crust. Because the earth is neither growing nor shrinking, addition of new crust at spreading zones means destruction of crust elsewhere. In areas of collision between ocean plates and continental plates, ocean crust bends under continental crust and slides back into the mantle.

This collision—or *subduction*—is happening right now along Alaska's southern shore, including lands under the St. Elias Range. The continental North American plate forces two to three inches (six and a half centimeters) of oceanic Pacific plate into the 26,000-foot-deep (7,925-m) Aleutian Trench each year. Far below, subducting Pacific plate material melts back into the mantle.

Mud volcanos

Mountain Building

Plate activity leaves a few telltale signs around the globe. The term *tectonics*, derived from the Greek word for "carpenter" or "builder," was not chosen on a whim. Obvious marks of tectonic activity in the Bordercountry include the Wrangell volcanos, the Chugach and St. Elias mountain ranges, the Shakwak valley, and earthquakes—the ultimate rock-and-roll dance.

After a subducting plate material melts into magma, it starts to rise through fissures and cracks in solid material. If magma breaks the surface, it erupts as lava through vents we call volcanos.

Over the last twenty-five million years, lava eruptions formed Mounts Sanford, Drum, Blackburn, Wrangell, and the other Wrangell volcanos. Today only Mount Wrangell, named "Uk'eledi" ("Smoking Top") by Athabaskans, is actively smoking. Thermal springs called *mud volcanos* near the flanks of Mount Drum indicate that things are still hot down below.

Steam vents on top of Mount Wrangell

Other mountains in the Bordercountry formed from a different method of tectonic carpentry. As land masses collide on moving plates, they wrinkle. Heaviest crumpling occurs at direct collision points. One such collision point is the St. Elias Mountains towering three vertical miles (4.8 km) over the Gulf of Alaska. Other wrinkles translate into the rugged Chugach, Mentasta, Nutzotin, and Kluane ranges.

Faults and Earthquakes

Bordercountry earthquakes are another reminder that geology is not a science of the past. Earth stretches and contracts at plate contact zones, sending waves of energy we feel as tremors and shakes.

Think of riding a bicycle down a bumpy gravel hill. You grip the handlebars as the bike and your body absorb one jolt after another. These jolts are similar to the vibrations of an earthquake after energy is released through volcanic eruptions and plate movement.

Rock bodies dropping and slipping along fractures in the earth called *faults* are the most common cause of earthquakes. Faults crisscross the Bordercountry. One of the most active faults in the area is the Totschunda Fault running from the Mentasta Mountains through the Wrangells and across the border into the Yukon Territory's Duke Depression. Rock masses along the Totschunda Fault slip against one another. Geologists estimate this fault has been storing compression energy for sixteen hundred years and sooner or later could be the site of a major earthquake. Unfortunately, seismology is not at present an exact science. No one really knows when Earth might decide to shake the North up a bit.

The St. Elias-Fairweather Fault running through the Chugach, St. Elias, and Fairweather mountains is the site of frequent jolts. A seismograph in Kluane's Haines Junction Visitor Centre records an average of three tremors per day along the fault system. Not surprising, really. Geologists believe the St. Elias-Fairweather fault system is the contact zone between the Pacific and North American plates. If Earth wants to stretch, this is where she is likely to do it.

The Denali fault system curves across all of southern Alaska and the Yukon, including the Bordercountry. Although movement along this fault currently displaces only .5 to 1.5 inches (1.3 to 3.8 cm) of continent per year, geological studies indicate rock masses have traveled over 200 miles (322 km) along the fault in the last thirty to one hundred million years. Even at the present snail's pace, North America's second highest mountain, Mount Logan (19,850 feet/6,050 m), is inching from Kluane toward Wrangell-St. Elias. Mount Logan has approximately one million years to get its papers in order for the border crossing.

Terranes

If you are not convinced by now that "terra firma" is a misnomer, consider this: Many geologists believe that Alaska and the Yukon as we know them did not exist two hundred million years ago. In a striking reflection of North America's cultural history, much of western Canada and the United States originated elsewhere, accreted to the continent, and changed forever the face of native lands.

The geological theory that the Bordercountry is composed of pieces of land from other places is a hot debate in the current world of rock study. Since the late 1970s, geologists have asserted that Alaska and the Yukon are comprised of over fifty dissimilar land masses called *terranes*. Each terrane has a rock and fossil history distinct from that of its neighbors and is bounded by major faults.

Terranes are the hobos of tectonics, hitching rides on the moving trains of continental and oceanic plates. Some terranes have made longer journeys than others. Wrangellia, one of the most studied terranes in the Bordercountry, probably migrated from within fifteen degrees north or south of the equator to its present location at sixty degrees north. These seasoned travellers are named *exotic* or *suspect terranes* in recognition of their foreign origins.

A tectonics map of the Bordercountry resembles the efforts of a novice quilter. Eight-odd trapezoids, triangles, rectangles, and assorted curious shapes suture together along clumsy fault seams.

The terrane quilt of the Bordercountry makes our human insistence on straight line boundaries look rather foolish. Tetlin Refuge includes parts of the Yukon-Tanana, Pingston, Windy-McKinley, and Gravina-Nutzotin terranes. Wrangell-St. Elias Park shares the Yukon-Tanana and Gravina-Nutzotin terranes with the Tetlin Refuge, and the Chugach, Alexander, Gravina-Nutzotin, and Wrangellia terranes with Kluane Park. The Yakutat terrane edges the maritime boundary of the Wrangell-St. Elias Park. None of these terranes originated in their current locations.

Some of the oldest rocks in Alaska and the Yukon comprise the Yukon-Tanana terrane. The rocks of the terrane probably accumulated six hundred to eight hundred million years ago as mud and sand along the margin of what would become North America. Over time these deposits hardened into rock. About two hundred million years ago the terrane drifted north and attached to the North American continent. Under intense pressure and heat during accretion, the terrane's rocks deformed into striped and folded stones.

Wrangellia tells a very different tale. About three hundred million years ago, not long after the first reptiles appeared on earth, Wrangellia rose as an arc of volcanic islands near the equator. For millions of years magma from subducting plates rose and erupted as lava through Wrangellia's volcanic vents. Plate activity changed and the volcanos cooled. Winds and water chiseled at Wrangellia's mountains and shores; the great arc of islands slowly subsided beneath the ocean. Millions of tiny marine animal skeletons and colorful corals layered over the eroded arc. About 245 million years ago, Wrangellia drifted over a spreading zone on the ocean floor. Flowing lavas raised the arc once again.

Wave-swept beach with the Wrangell-St. Elias Mountains in the background

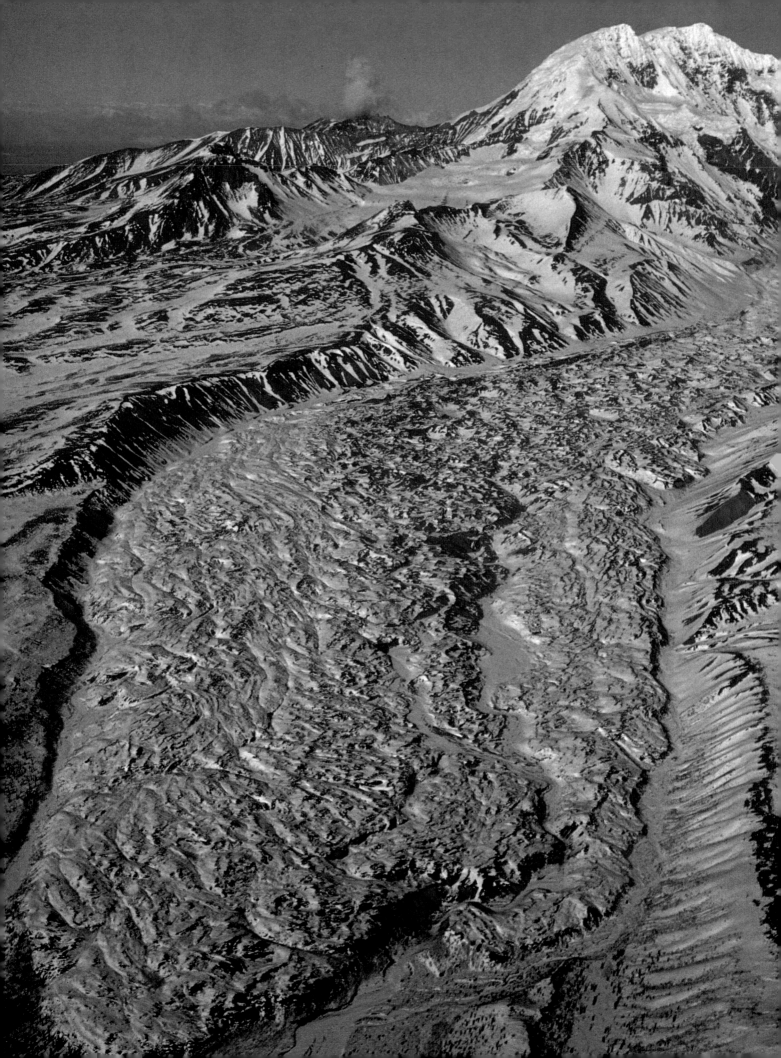

This history of subsidence and growth produced the Chitistone limestone and volcanic Nicolai greenstone formations visible throughout the Wrangells today. Mineral solutions including copper and silver migrated through these rocks and solidified into major deposits later mined at the famous Kennecott Mines. Other solutions migrated through Bordercountry terranes to produce the seductive glint of gold.

Formation of the Bordercountry

Some two hundred million years ago, Wrangellia encountered an older volcanic island arc with a similar history of destruction and resurrection. This older arc, known as the Alexander terrane, formed five hundred million years ago. Wrangellia and the Alexander terrane collided. The meeting of these two set off literal fireworks as volcanos blew and covered both terranes. The joined terranes rafted north on predecessors to today's Pacific plate. During the journey another terrane, the Gravina-Nutzotin, jumped aboard, layering over Wrangellia and Alexander.

Fifty million years later another terrane, the Peninsular, joined the raft. The amalgamated Wrangellia-Alexander-Peninsular-Gravina-Nutzotin terranes, having earned the title "Superterrane," continued northward on ocean plates. Sediments eroding from the superterrane fanned across the ocean floor on strong submarine currents. Over time the sediments hardened into the beginning of the Chugach terrane.

The Superterrane met the North American continent some 125 million years ago, not long after the first birds flew earth's skies. Volcanos heralded the event with great eruptions of glowing lava ropes and fiery molten bombs.

Docking near present-day northern California and Oregon, the Superterrane made a temporary stop, then slipped north up the edge of the continent, leaving slivers of Wrangellia in Oregon and British Columbia in its wake.

Between eighty and twenty-five million years ago the combined Wrangellia, Alexander, Gravina-Nutzotin, and Chugach terranes halted, forming the Bordercountry. Smaller terranes, including Pingston and Windy-McKinley, were sandwiched between the Yukon-Tanana terrane and pieces of the mighty Superterrane. Lands crumpled, hills rose, volcanos formed, seas rushed in. And more was to come.

Yet another terrane, the Yakutat, broke off the continent near present-day southeastern Alaska and moved north. Lava erupted from the Wrangell volcanos with the Yakutat terrane movement.

About fifteen million years ago, pressure from the Yakutat terrane pushed the Chugach and St. Elias mountains skyward. Approximately twelve million years ago, glaciers formed on the high peaks.

The Yakutat terrane docked against the coast some five million years ago. The western Wrangell volcanos, including Mounts Drum, Sanford, and Wrangell, formed in response. Great blocks dropped along fault lines, creating Kluane's Shakwak Trench.

Lava flowed thick over the next 4-5 million years, filling the area surrounding the Copper Basin and sending tremendous mudslides down the Copper Valley. With a change in plate movement about two hundred thousand years ago, the Wrangell volcanos quieted. The last significant Wrangell eruptions occurred approximately ten thousand years ago, although as recently as 1,250 years ago, ash from a volcano near Mount Bona in the St. Elias mountains fell over much of the Bordercountry. Residents of Chitina, Alaska, reported fire from Mount Wrangell in 1930.

A critical principle of earth time is that change is the only constant. Right now the Yakutat terrane is docking against the Gulf Coast of Alaska, raising the St. Elias peaks by over one inch (2.5 cm) per year. Mount Wrangell is smoking, lands along faults are sliding. The cycle of creation and destruction continues.

Rocks

Rocks are the fingerprints of the earth, leaving clues to the tectonic story of terranes. Geologists can pick up a rock and decipher earth history from information recorded in the rock's crystals, texture, color, weight, cleavage planes, imbedded fossils, and magnetic materials.

Despite the many colors, shapes, and sizes of rocks, they all are just variations on a theme of three: igneous, metamorphic, and sedimentary. Igneous rock forms from cooled molten material. Metamorphic rocks do as their name suggests: They change through heat and pressure from one kind of rock to another. Sedimentary rocks are fragments of other rocks brought together through wind and water transport.

The three types of rocks twirl round and round in earth time: the cliche' "what goes around comes around" explains the rock cycle in five words. In one example, molten material moves through overlying rock and slowly cools to igneous rock within the earth's crust. Erosion processes—including wind, frost, and water—wear away at surface material, eventually exposing the igneous rock. As the surface rock crumbles and is carried away, it compacts into sedimentary rock.

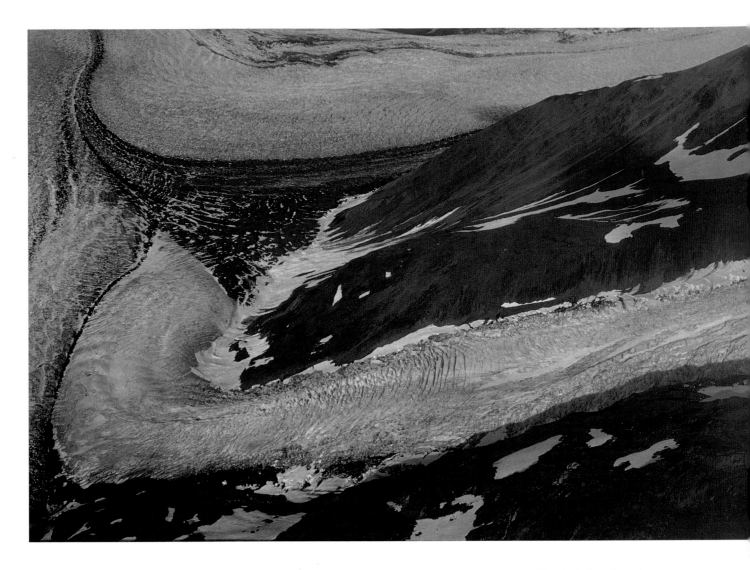

Over time, the sedimentary rock is deposited in submarine trenches. In the trenches, earth forces heat and pressurize the rock, changing its chemical composition and texture from sedimentary to metamorphic. Perhaps the rock is pushed back into the earth's mantle. It then becomes molten and the cycle begins again.

Hubbard Glacier tributaries

Glaciers

Groaning, cracking blue ice; meltwater dribbling and rushing down crystal walls; rock-covered ice undulating in earth time; snow and rock swirling in marbleized sheets; columns of blue ice breaking, crashing into deep salty waters; blinding white throwing light back at the sun.

The carnival of tectonic activity brought exotic rocks to the Bordercountry from points around the world. Like all carnival workers, rocks never stay in one

place for long. In the Bordercountry, glaciers are one of the most common modes of travel.

If plate tectonics is a Bordercountry builder, glaciers are the refining sculptors. Glaciers carve wide U-shaped valleys, mountain-high amphitheaters, and ridges as sharp as eagle talons. Nowhere in the world is the work of glaciers more evident than in the Bordercountry.

Ice Movement

Rivers of ice have flowed down south Alaska and Yukon peaks for about thirteen million years. During the recent Ice Age—between two million and ten thousand years ago—most of the North was under thousands of feet of ice.

Glaciers advanced through the Wrangells to cover the Tetlin Refuge south of the Black Hills, leaving rolling mounds of rock and Jatahmund Lake in retreat. Refuge lands farther north and west remained an ice-free corridor important to animal and human migration.

Ice blanketed the Kluane and Wrangell-St. Elias parks area, creating the crags, valleys, and fjords we see today. To get an idea of the height of these former oceans of ice, look at the shape of a Bordercountry mountain. The jagged peaks were above ice, the rounded mountains underneath.

Glaciers also changed the drainage patterns of many rivers, including the mighty Yukon. Before the time of ice, the upper Yukon River flowed south on a 189 mile (304 km) course through the channels of the Alsek River to enter the Gulf of Alaska near Yakutat. As ice sheets blocked access to the southern route, the Yukon shifted directions to flow northwest and took the drainages of surrounding rivers with it. Today the Yukon and its tributaries travel over 1,300 miles (2,092 km) to the Bering Sea. The Tanana River may have pulled a similar trick, stealing Tetlin area drainages from the White River.

As you drive through the Copper River valley, imagine the entire basin filled with water ten thousand years ago. This was Glacial Lake Ahtna, a glacier-dammed lake that covered over two thousand square miles. Silt deposits still can be spotted on valley walls. Scuba gear would also have been essential equipment in visiting the Kluane Visitor's Centre in Haines Junction twelve thousand years ago. Glacial Lake Champagne, another aquatic consequence of glacial movement, covered the site of the town with 500 feet (152 meters) of icy water.

Things warmed up seven thousand years ago during a period known as the "Thermal Maximum." Bordercountry glaciers dried up: There is more ice in the area today.

Temperatures dropped again about 5,500 years ago, and the "Neoglacial" or "Little Ice Age" began. Glaciers marched forward, repeatedly blocking Kluane's Alsek River and creating the 60-mile-long, 120-mile-deep (97-km-long and 193-km-deep) Neoglacial Lake Alsek. Once again Haines Junction went for a swim. A smaller version of this lake formed in 1953 and could form again if Lowell Glacier blocks the wild Alsek.

Glacier-dammed lakes, or *jokulhlaups*, still form throughout the Bordercountry. Hidden Lake near McCarthy drains annually through a 10-mile (16-km) subglacial channel, often surprising visitors camping next to the Kennicott River.

Just three to four hundred years ago, an advance of the Kaskawulsh Glacier blocked Kluane Lake's southern drainage to the Alsek River. In response, Kluane Lake cut a northern channel to join the Yukon River's trek to the Bering Sea. Geologists believe unpredictable Kluane Lake might someday return to its southern route.

Some of the glacier headliners in the world today lie along the coast of the Wrangell-St. Elias Park. Icy Bay, now five miles wide and twenty-six miles long (eight km wide and nearly 42 km long), was completely under ice as recently as 1904. The glacier receded twenty-five miles (forty kilometers) in eighty years, backing up at an average annual speed of 1,500 feet (457 meters).

Ninety-two-mile (148-km) long Hubbard Glacier, current record holder for longest North American valley glacier, filled all of Yakutat Bay a thousand years ago. In 1986 Hubbard advanced across the entrance to Russell Fjord, creating Glacial Russell Lake. Five months later, the ice dam burst. Water moving thirty-five times faster than the flow of Niagara Falls roared through the ice, resculpting the surrounding coast. The changed landscape is but a variation of events repeated on countless occasions throughout earth time.

During the Ice Age, glaciers covered half of Alaska and much of the Yukon. Today, only five percent of Alaska is still glaciated, but fifty percent of the Wrangell-St. Elias and Kluane parks remain under the slow flow of ice rivers. The Tetlin Refuge is glacier free.

Glacier ABCs

How do glaciers flow? Go to the freezer and pull out an ice cube. Put the cube on the counter. In a very short time, a thin layer of water will have melted between the bottom of the ice and the countertop. Now push the cube. See how easily it slides on the lubricating water? You are watching a mechanism of glacier movement.

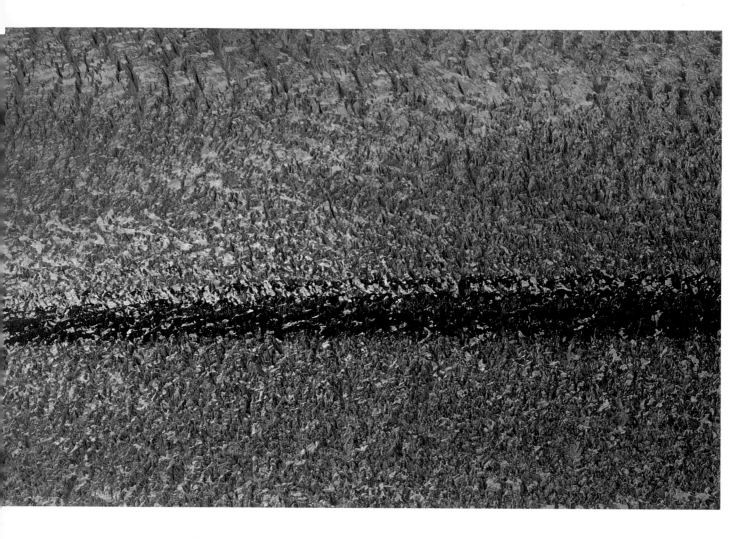

Glacier art
(preceding page) Hubbard Glacier

Ice is just another form of metamorphic rock. Six-armed snow crystals accumulate and begin to change into a rounded shape in a few days. Snow surviving a summer melt season becomes *firn*, an intermediate stage in which pore space between granules is eliminated. Firn eventually becomes glacial ice impermeable to air. Water molecules absorb all colors of the spectrum except blue, giving glaciers a soft bluish tint. The force of gravity and accumulating snow pushes the glaciers down mountain slopes.

Glacial anatomy tells us something about the wisdom of giving way to avoid cracking up. Ice rivers are divided into a plastic underlayer and a brittle surface. As a glacier moves, the flexible layer flows over obstacles, conforms to topographical changes, and winds to its destination. The brittle layer responds to stresses by cracking open. These breaks, or *crevasses*, may yawn tens of feet wide and deep.

Many of us also would benefit from adopting glacier accounting principles. A glacier has an accumulation area in its upper zone, a loss area in its lower zone, and an equilibrium line marking the area where net loss equals net gain. Accumulation occurs with snowfall. Loss is through melting and the *calving* (breaking off) of ice columns. A glacier is neither a borrower nor a lender: It advances if accumulation is greater than loss, recedes if loss is greater than accumulation, and remains stationary if neither gain nor loss predominates.

Sometimes glaciers move forward quickly, between ten and one hundred times their normal speed. Glaciologists have termed these sprinters *surging glaciers* and suspect release of subglacial meltwater as the power behind the push. For an unknown reason, surging glaciers are concentrated in certain areas. The Bordercountry is a favored location; almost two hundred can be found in the St. Elias range.

Glaciers and Sculpture in the Parks

Ice in the Bordercountry comes in many varieties, including *icefields, piedmonts, cirques, valleys, fjords,* and *tidewater* glaciers. An icefield is a large interconnected area of alpine glaciers. The world's largest nonpolar icefield is in the St. Elias Icefield Range. Malaspina Glacier, a piedmont glacier—or area of connected valley glaciers—is the size of Rhode Island.

Cirque glaciers are circular glacial depressions on mountainsides and abound in the parks. Hubbard and Nabesna valley glaciers are two of the world's largest ice rivers flowing into mountain valleys. The coastal area of the Wrangell-St. Elias Park boasts fjord glaciers that occupy submerged coastal valleys and tidewater glaciers that terminate in ocean waters.

Not every glacier is a field of ice. *Rock glaciers*—a curious variation on the ice glacier—are composed of rocks interlaced with ice not visible on the surface. The sediment layers insulate the ice core, protecting it from melting. Rock glaciers move in the same manner as ice glaciers. There are many rock glaciers in the Bordercountry, including one just above the Kennecott Mine.

Glacial landscapes are glimpses into raw creation. When the walls of ice roll back, we have an opportunity to see how land and life evolve and change . . . only to change again. Glaciologist and naturalist John Muir said it best:

> *Standing here, with facts so fresh and telling and held up so vividly before us, every seeing observer, not to say geologist, must readily apprehend the earth-sculpturing, landscape-making action of flowing ice. And here, too, one learns that the world, though made, is yet being made; that this is the morning of creation. . .*[1]

[1]*Muir, John,* Travels in Alaska. *1915. (San Francisco: Sierra Club Books 1988) 56-57.*

Glaciers scrape, tug, carry, and dump rock materials in shaping lands. Considered by scientists to be the earth's most efficient erosion agent, glaciers know their business. At its headwall, or *bergschrund*, a glacier plucks large pieces of rock from the mountainside to create a bowl-shape characteristic of cirques.

As they scrape and grind against mountain walls, ice rivers leave oversteep walls prone to landslides and long scratches called *glacial striations*. Cirques carved on opposite sides of a mountain slope create sheer serrated ridges known as *aretes*. Three or more cirque glaciers on one peak sculpt a pyramid-like horn.

Nor do glaciers leave their host valleys as they found them. Narrow valleys are widened to a deep U-shape with steep or sloping walls.

Water and ice carry quarried and fallen rocks on the sides, middle, surface, and at the base. Swirling streams of meltwater haul house-sized boulders and penny-sized pebbles down stripes of gray interlocked with blue ice fingers. Generally known as *moraines*, these sediment stripes are called *lateral* moraines when on glacial sidewalls, *medial* moraines when in the middle of two joined glaciers, and *terminal* moraines when dumped or pushed in front of the farthest forward reach of a glacier's snout. Look for moraines on the Kennicott Glacier when visiting the Kennecott Mine in the Wrangell-St. Elias Park area.

As you squint through binoculars at a far ridge to look for signs of glacial sculpting, remember to look under your feet. The rocks that glacier toted from near and far had to end up somewhere. You may be walking on them. Malaspina Glacier's terminal moraines have been in place so long that trees tall enough to pique the interest of logging companies now stretch up from the fertile till.

If you learn to read them, the lands around you may tell a story of glacial sculpting. That rounded lake may be a *kettle lake*, formed from a chunk of ice left behind as ice receded. The long narrow knoll snaking across the valley floor may be an *esker*, a deposit left by subglacial streams. Those strange hills steep on one side and gently sloping on the other may be *drumlins*, another form of subglacial deposit. The Toyota-sized boulder sitting in the middle of nowhere probably is an *erratic* dropped off by a glacier. That dust you brush from your eyes may be *rock flour*, glacially ground sediment transported by wind.

Other Sculptors

Glaciers may be the most obvious carvers, but other erosion artists labor to pull Bordercountry mountains down. Whether a whispering breeze or howling gale, wind works constantly to transport sediment and carve rock faces. In some places, including the Donjek Valley in Kluane or along the Alaska Highway near

Sunlit stream

Alsek River in Kluane
National Park Reserve

the Tetlin Refuge, winds have built dunes of glacial flour, or *loess*. In other places, including Bonanza Peak above the Kennecott Mines in Wrangell-St. Elias Park, winds chisel faces into soaring limestone spires.

Permafrost, or permanently frozen ground, is a significant Bordercountry sculptor. In the Tetlin Refuge, black spruce stands cover much of the ground and insulate permafrost to a depth of 200 feet (61 m) deep. When a layer of permafrost melts on hillsides, overlying ground slumps into gentle lobes. Spruce roots are not able to penetrate permafrost, and their shallow support structures cannot hold the trees upright. These tilted forests are affectionately known as "drunken forests."

Water and temperature work in tandem to move rocks with the single-mindedness of an ant hauling a breadcrumb. Water seeps into rock cracks, then freezes, expands, and cleaves shards from stone faces. Over time, this action produces sharp rocky fields of *talus*, the nemesis of many a hiker.

Rivers and streams are another great shaper of lands. Most of the rivers in the Bordercountry are milky, churning glacial waters. Transporting materials from glaciers to ocean, rivers both carve lands and dump sediment into great deltas.

Kluane has two major drainage systems, the Yukon and the Alsek Rivers. Kaskawulsh Glacier meltwater flows north through the Slims River and Kluane Lake to the Yukon. Kaskawulsh glacier waters also flow south through the Kaskawulsh and Dezadeash rivers to the untamed Alsek.

Only the Alsek and Copper rivers still flow to the Gulf of Alaska. No other Bordercountry rivers were able to carve down as fast as the Chugach and St. Elias ranges rose up. The Copper River drains most of the Wrangell-St. Elias Park, with help from the Chitina River. Glacial in origin, the Chitina and the Copper carry some of the highest sediment loads of any river in North America.

The Wrangell Mountains also drain north through the Nabesna and Chisana rivers to the Tanana River bordering the Tetlin Refuge and to the White River in the Wrangell-St. Elias Park. Both the Tanana and the White rivers wind their way to the Yukon River and then make the long journey to the Bering Sea.

Carving, digging, flowing hauling, breaking, building. An unending dance of birth and death, creation and destruction: the flux of earth time.

The morning was overcast, gray with dark clouds and feathery mist. The smell of fall was heavy in the air, earthy and rich. I was up early in hopes of photographing Dall sheep in morning sunlight. For an hour I had been grazing with two young ewes, waiting for the light. I sampled blueberries while the sheep munched on a variety of grasses and sedges. As they foraged they kept an eye on me much as they would on the wolves with whom they shared this plateau. I kept a respectful distance.

Settling onto a rocky perch, I waited for the sun, contemplating the beauty and wildness of the Chitistone Gorge. A ray of light escaped through a break in the clouds, highlighting my surroundings and taking my breath away. As the clouds lifted, the landscape emerged. I was surrounded by snow-capped peaks, glaciers, the reds and yellows of alpine tundra in fall, and, of course, the gorge. Chitistone Gorge combines the red rock beauty of southern Utah with the rawness of Alaska. Near the head of the gorge, the Chitistone River becomes a spectacular waterfall plunging into the river valley a thousand feet (three hundred meters) below. It takes only a little imagination to see and feel mountains being etched, valleys being sculpted, nature at its most creative.

All this activity makes for challenging foot travel. On the hike in, I passed a recent landslide the size of a city block. It was as if half a mountain had fallen, taking out trees, rerouting the river, and leaving a golden ten-ton (nine-metric-ton) rock at river's edge.

Backcountry travel in the region is not for everyone. Raging rivers, variable weather, few trails, no trail markers, rough terrain, and dense undergrowth make most backcountry trips true wilderness experiences. The rivers themselves are perhaps the most challenging aspect of backcountry travel. During the peak of snow melt and after major storms, many streams become impossible to cross or are crossable only early in the morning, when water levels are usually at their lowest. Many destinations in the park, including the Chitistone area, are accessible only by air, due to difficult river crossings. Air taxi services operate out of Tok, Gulkana, Nabesna, and McCarthy.

A camp overlooking the Chitistone River Valley in Wrangell-St. Elias National Park

My trip to the Chitistone Gorge had begun seven days before at the Gulkana airstrip. We spent the first four days camping in the rain at the airstrip waiting for the weather to clear. Our plans were to hike part of the historic Chitistone Trail from Skolai Pass down the Goat Trail to the Chitistone Gorge, across the glacier and out along the Chitistone River to the Glacier Creek airstrip, where we would be picked up. The Goat Trail section of the hike is appropriately named due to the steep scree slopes one traverses. Dall sheep rather than goats are seen along the trail. "Trail" is actually a misnomer, for on many sections of the hike there is no distinct trail at all. Use of the Chitistone Trail dates back to Athabaskan hunting and trading parties and to miners traveling to the Chisana gold rush in 1912 and 1913.

Our flight in is white-knuckles rough. We bounce our way through Skolai Pass, our drop-off location, as wind and turbulence make it impossible to land. Switching to "plan two," we decide to try to land at Glacier Creek and hike up the Goat Trail, returning to Glacier Creek for pick-up. Fortunately, the Glacier Creek airstrip is more protected, and we are able to land.

Now after three days of hiking up rock-strewn river drainages, fording thigh-deep glacial streams, and gingerly crossing the toe of the Chitistone Glacier, I am perched upon the edge of the Chitistone Gorge watching dawn unfold. My feet hurt from walking on rocky surfaces, my shoulders ache from carrying an eighty-pound (30 kg) pack overloaded with camera equipment, but I have rarely felt more content.

My hope is that this experience can be preserved for future generations of people, sheep, and wolves. As more people become aware of the Wrangell-St. Elias National Park through this book and others, there will be new pressures on this area and the region as a whole.

For all its ruggedness, the ecosystem is fragile. It is a demanding environment for even the hardiest plants and animals. Many species are at the northern extreme of their habitat. For others such as wolves and the grizzly bear, this expansive region is one of the few remaining wild ecosystems large enough to support their populations. Finding the balance to accommodate increased visitor usage while protecting the wildness of the park will be a challenge.

Jatahmund Lake in Tetlin National Wildlife Refuge

chapter three

LIFESTRANDS:
ECOLOGY

Waves crash against glacier ice; water plunges over a smooth granite ridge. Winds howl across a lake broad as the gray sky. Wolves watch a weakened Dall sheep struggle in deep snow. Trumpeter swans lift heavy wings to the horizon. Orca whales breech ocean waters. A lone hiker bends to touch the muddy print of a grizzly bear. The Alaska-Yukon Bordercountry. Home.

Ecology, ecosystems, and ecofriendly cleaning sprays. "Eco" is a marketable prefix in the late twentieth century, but what does it mean? Greek in origin, eco means "home." To study an ecosystem is to wonder about our home.

A scientist might explain that ecology is an examination of intertwining physical conditions and energy. Ecologists are synthesizers, combiners of mathematical formulas and marmot whistles. Why does the moss campion, a common tundra flower, resemble a couch cushion? Why does fire in the boreal forest support moose populations? And why do blueberries make themselves deliciously obvious to rooting bear?

Specialists tell us berries are a reproduction strategy. A percentage of seeds passes through the digestive system of a berry-loving ursine and roots to patches of ground. Favorable soils provide nutrients essential to growth and new berry bushes sprout. A successful species survival mechanism.

Science is but one way to understand ecology. Another is to walk the land. Traditional peoples of the Bordercountry have always understood that moose prefer the savory greens that sprout in a burned boreal forest. And that boiled willow tea eases pregnancy.

Scientists, subsistence harvesters, and soft path walkers all know: Life is woven in intricate webs. All of life. Including humans. Even humans who know more about subway systems than ecosystems. You are connected to the Bordercountry. Other places may be more familiar, less wild. But

Moonglow over Deadman Lake in Tetlin National Wildlife Refuge

Kluane National Park Reserve, Wrangell-St. Elias National Park, and the Tetlin National Wildlife Refuge are not unknown. They are part of your—our—collective Earth home.

Driving the Bordercountry, you may see barren rock and scrubby flatlands. A flight over the Kluane Icefields might only confirm an initial impression of desolation. Then you venture on a hike. Then your perspective changes.

Perhaps you stop at Kluane Sheep Mountain Visitor's Centre or the path along Deadman's Lake in the Tetlin Refuge. Maybe you take a turn up the Nabesna Road entrance to Wrangell-St. Elias. You stop the car. Stretching sleepy limbs, you climb out.

A sharp breeze stings open your eyes. Sage fills your nostrils. A small creature scurries from the vibration of your gait; Bell-shaped twinflowers and magenta stalks of fireweed spring from the crush of your footprint. A creek surges. Willows sway: Hairs rise on the back of your neck. Is it a bear? This country is alive, and you can feel it.

Understanding ecology requires a flexible definition of "boundary." Start by throwing away that map in your glove compartment. Better yet, unfold it and erase the international border between Kluane in Canada and Wrangell-St. Elias in the United States. Rub out lines dividing Tetlin Refuge from Wrangell-St. Elias. But leave lines distinguishing the parks-refuge Bordercountry from the rest of Alaska and the Yukon. Those lines promise a perimeter of protection around lands, plants, and animals within Kluane, Tetlin, and Wrangell-St. Elias.

Anything from the mud clump on the bottom of your hiking boot to the entire Tetlin Refuge is an ecosystem: a combination of land, climate, plants, and animals. And what about glaciers nourishing rivers watering lowlands filling with

Springtime in the Wrangells

White spruce in
Tetlin National Wildlife Refuge

salmon feeding bears? A larger ecosystem might include the mountains of the Wrangells, the St. Elias range, the icefields shared by Kluane and Wrangell-St. Elias, and the silty forelands melting into the Gulf of Alaska.

Wrangell glaciers also creak and crack to Chisana River headwaters. The Chisana rolls from Wrangell Mountains through the Tetlin Refuge. Lilypads, waterbugs, and flowing fish form ecosystems in rock-sheltered river pools. Aquatic Tetlin vegetation forms strands in a web weaving through birds migrating far beyond the Bordercountry. Ecosystem boundaries shrink and stretch.

Remember the fable of four blindfolded wisemen asked to identify an elephant? Picture the sages facing different parts of a moose: one at the rack, one at the tail, one along the moose rib cage, and one precariously close to a 70-pound (32-kg) foreleg. Upon examining the available ungulate section, each guru pictures a different creature. Unable to investigate the whole moose, none of the wisemen accurately describes the animal.

So it is with ecosystems. Parts are connected to wholes, and wholes to parts. Between Klukshu and Kennecott you may see woven eagle talons stretching across

68

a Chilkat Tlingit blanket or a strand of beaded forget-me-nots curving the edge of Athabaskan fur mittens. Take a close look, for these works of wearable art are human interpretations of Bordercountry ecosystems.

Each bead or wool strand is a distinct and singular whole. But beads and strands are also parts of larger designs. Single beads blend into jeweled flowers. Woven threads become stylized woolen raven eyes.

Relationships among plants and animals are as simple as a single bead, complex as a ceremonial dress design. One strand weaves into another, shapes and colors blend and separate.

Neighborhoods known in science as "habitats" form and change in a process called "succession." After fire in the Bordercountry, tasty morel mushrooms push through ash. Sways of fireweed splash pink against charred birch trunks. Wood-hungry bugs bore into burned bark. Woodpeckers drill for the tasty insects. Voles chew fresh forage. Poplar and aspen trees shoot upward. One hundred years later, tall white spruce stands will have crowded out smaller shade-intolerant poplars, and birds more suited to high nests will be trilling from the treetops.

The thread connecting parts to the whole is energy. What does a whitecapped wave churning across vast Kluane Lake have in common with moose browsing on Nabesna Road willow, evergreen leaves of the leatherleaf plant, and your breakfast pancakes? Answer: Energy.

Cycles of life depend on the manufacture and efficient use of energy. The sun sends 1,300,000,000,000,000,000,000,000 calories of energy to earth every year. Plants capture about one percent of that energy through photosynthesis, a chemical process that converts light to sugar and starches.

Plants form the base of a "House-that-Jack-built" pyramid that ecologists use to explain the web of lifestrands. Plant-eating animals occupy the middle tiers of energy consumption models. Species closer to the apex of the pyramid also eat meat. These omnivores and carnivores require more energy to support fewer lives than species closer to the base. It really is more lonely at the top.

Ecology reveals that life depends on death. A muskrat chews life from succulent duckgrass. A red fox kills the muskrat and

Timber wolf

An alert red fox

moves on to find another meal. Small carnivores and insects tear flesh from the remains of the carcass, leaving the rest to decompose into soil-enriching nutrients. Over time, green shoots push through the desiccated skeleton. And so the cycle goes.

Through evolutionary experiments, species craft interdependent modes of survival. Over tens of thousands of human-measured years, slight genetic mutations become survival mechanisms.

Quaking aspen and other deciduous trees go through an annual "hardening process" to transform sap to antifreeze. Sea-faring cormorants dry wings on the wind, seals give birth to pups on floating icebergs. Snowshoe hares hide, turning summer brown fur to winter white and back again. Tundra flowers assume parabolic shapes to focus heat and lure pollinators. Dall sheep climb up and down mountainsides to maximize summer grasses and minimize winter starvation. No single method of energy cycling is "best." The only test is whether a species continues to survive.

The Bordercountry is vast: tidewater glaciers to sand dunes, sea level to 19,000 feet (5,800 m), annual temperatures ranging between -70-degrees F and 90-degrees F (-57-degrees C and 32-degrees C). In testimony to tenacity, life colonizes every Wrangells-St. Elias, Kluane, and Tetlin crack, crevice, and creek. Energy lifestrands link coastal Sitka spruce with pika haypiles on mountain ridges and migrating sandhill cranes resting on muskeg.

A hallmark of Bordercountry habitats is the *taiga*, or boreal forest. Taiga is from a Russian word meaning "little sticks." An afternoon driving the Alaska Highway or a single glance at a boreal photograph will convince you that the Russians had a way with descriptive phrasing.

Like most travelers, however, the Russians had limited exposure to the lands they named "little sticks." They saw the boreal forest as merely lots-of-cold-swamps-and-sorry-looking-trees, poor cousins to rich mineral veins and azure-tinted ice cones. But the taiga is an elegant life design in a challenging environment.

Northern taiga and muskeg balance water and vegetation, creating homes for geese, swans, bear, moose, and freshwater fish. Two feet under bog, the ground is permanently frozen. Yet plants, trees, and animals have developed ways to survive. Black spruce spread their roots horizontally. Some plants, including the sundew, have learned to eat meat. Shaped like a closed eyelid, sundews are the Venus fly traps of the North. Opalescent dew beading tips of the sundew's eyelash-curved filaments is actually sticky poison capable of melting bugs into dinner entrees.

The bogs of the taiga also create a combustible plant fuel called *peat*. Over thousands of years, thousands of leaves from thousands of plants crush one another and foliage becomes fuel. Bricks of dried peat have heated many a Bordercountry fire.

Few visitors to the Bordercountry will see its marine habitats, but the coastal waters of Wrangell-St. Elias are filled with life. Icy Bay, deglaciated only one hundred years ago, is home to Steller sea lions, harbor seals, marbled murrelets, and whales. Some of the rarest coastal rainforest in the world stretches along the mineral-rich Malaspina Glacier forelands.

Boreal forest in autumn in Tetlin National Wildlife Refuge

Endings

Equally remote are the thriving populations on island peaks in the glacial ocean of the Kluane and Wrangell-St. Elias icefields. Ice-free peaks jutting from St. Elias icefields are called *nunataks*, which means "lonely ones" in the language of the Inuit.

Some believe nunatak plants and animals have perched on rocky outposts for as long as ice has veiled the Bordercountry. Life here is streamlined. Sprinkles of potentilla flowers balancing on knife-edged ridges waste no energy on showy blossoms when clean lines will do. Residents are also less choosy about food sources: Unlike mainland relatives, some nunatak pika add dead animal finds to their usual vegetarian haypile stacks.

Each ecosystem moves in cycles tuned to time and conditions. Over ten-year periods lynx, snowshoe hare, and willows weave abundance, starvation, and equilibrium in different tensions.

Winter-white bunnies nip exposed willow bush ends. If enough branches become rabbit fodder, snowshoe hare may increase their population. When rabbit numbers become high enough to threaten willow survival, the plants start to exude a toxin to discourage further bunny bites. As rabbits find less food, their numbers decrease. Simultaneously, lynx grown fat on snowbunny meat start to starve.

With fewer rabbits, the willow produce tasty nibbles again. With fewer lynx, the snowshoe hare begin to dot more snowbanks. And the circle turns.

Fire is a common mechanism of habitat change in the Bordercountry. Smokey the Bear taught many of us that forest fires are destructive. So they can be. But fires also recycle stagnant energy into flows of life. Athabaskan hunters used controlled burns to encourage visits from edibles, mushroom to moose.

Science agrees with traditional practices. Cyclic natural burns chemically enrich forest ecosystems. Pioneer communities of fireweed, poplar, and alder fix soil with nitrogen, phosphorous, and other vital nutrients. Moose frequent postfire intermediate communities of willow and alder.

72

Bordercountry residents make sharp trades with extreme environments to ensure survival. Flies land on bowl-shaped tundra plants to gain reflective radiation and inadvertently distribute pollen. Cupped flowers barter warmth for DNA transport, gambling species survival on an inviting sundeck. Lower elevation flies are less likely to freeze midsummer but might stick to a sundew lash. Which fly species has the better life strategy? Time may tell.

Scientists have learned certain general adaptation rules about northern mammals. Compare a drawing or photograph of foxes living in Yosemite and the Yukon. Not only are their fur coats of different color, but the northern fox have smaller ears and paws. Why? Smaller appendages survive better in freezing temperatures. And white fur hairs are hollow, trapping an extra "kilowatt" of energy.

Animal size also affects winter survival strategies. A mammal smaller than a snowshoe hare cannot stay active and above ground during winter unless meat is on the menu. Smaller animals need more energy to stay warm than available plant foods can provide. So herbivorous ground squirrels sleep, and carnivorous six-inch (15-cm) weasels stay awake.

Every Bordercountry traveller meets the arctic ground squirrel. This critter seems to be experimenting with exploitation of human emotion as a reliable food source, so watch your backpack. One moment this fat squirrel is a photogenic friend, and the next he is gnawing on your plastic baggie labeled "Breakfast No. 3."

Like humans, bears occupy the apex of an energy pyramid. Bears gobble energy in a one-to-ten ratio to vegetarian animals. Translation: Bears (and humans) are the vacuum cleaners of energy consumption.

The omnivorous bear eats berries, roots, plants, arctic ground squirrel, moose, and just about anything else it can find. Bears are not always energy efficient in seeking grub. They may dig down a camp-robbing gopher tunnel for longer than mathematical energy loss formulae would advise. Perhaps squirrely chitter-chatter just gets on bear nerves.

Arctic ground squirrels and bears share the fat-and-quiet approach to winter. Mammals small and large practice forms of hibernation to survive the cold season. Squirrels sleep soundly, but contrary to popular belief, bears wake now and again. If spring temperatures are unusually warm, a bear may rise early and leave the den.

Imagine a camera in a bear den on an early spring day. Cornsilk-colored light streams in through the dank tunnel. Dripping earth walls encircle the bear's matted brown fur. Licking white incisors, she stretches. Her nose pushes through jagged crystals; with a deep breath she pulls fresh air into her lungs. Should she get up? A gamble that winter is over may have deathly consequences if the cold returns and snow veils food sources.

Warm-blooded critters easily capture human attention. Nature films of sharp-ribbed winter moose bowing to wind-waves of snow are dramatic. But what of two-inch (5-cm) tundra moss campion buried in moose-sized snowbanks? Plants also have evolved ways to live in the Bordercountry.

Tundra plants such as the pink-bellied moss campion may be the most insistent energy on earth. Moss campion is a bushy cushion with fingernail-sized blossoms. The plant's round, low profile is efficient in high-mountain conditions hostile to tall shade-producing vegetation. From a distance, mounds of low tundra plants sometimes are indistinguishable from dark rocks. On closer examination campion and other tundra blossoms are vegetative effusions.

The low round shape is favored in the high country for wind protection and warmth. If you gently placed a thermometer in the middle of a midsummer campion bush, you would find that the interior of the plant is significantly warmer than prevailing air. Talk about heat retention: If only winter sleeping bags were as effective.

Plants have differing reproductive strategies. Some grow extremely fast to sow seeds before autumn. Others accumulate energy in roots for years, then burst into dramatic bloom.

A wooly lousewort saves energy for four years to produce a single flower. Growing low to the ground in typical tundra style, the lousewort blooms are Gulliver-large and far out-size their Lilliputian stems. Louseworts are shaped, colored, and formed to attract the attention of specific insect species. The lousewort spends it all to attract a pollinator.

An energy-seeking bumblebee may alight and be dusted with lousewort pollen. Perhaps that bee will fly to another bud and brush dusty pollen across another lousewort pistil. And maybe, just maybe, seeds will find fertile soil, survive, and mature to begin again.

Lousewort survival strategy may not always be the same. Perhaps a few lousewort seeds will produce a different scent, one more attractive to pollinators. Perhaps the lousewort is negotiating between adaptation and extinction.

Avoiding typical Bordercountry boom and bust, many northern plants sacrifice broad deciduous leaf baskets for slim structures able to harvest light year-round. Plants five inches (13 cm) high are as "evergreen" as a yuletide Scotch pine.

Consider the common leatherleaf. Any visitor to the Bordercountry has seen this waxy sprout: Small leaves, hairy stem, urn-shaped flowers . . . At first blush, leatherleaf may seem beneath notice, just another spindly form with furry veined leaves. Neither rare nor exotic. Any sharp-eyed traveler can find it.

Leatherleaf is a member of the heather family, a clan suited to subarctic temperature extremes. Leatherleaf's ordinariness belies its extraordinary ability to live.

This small plant turns sunlight into food and survives annual temperature swings of 150 degrees F (65 degrees C). Its leaves curl under to protect breathing holes from ice-coated winds and its flowers retain heat in curved centers. Evergreen appendages coax energy from thin winter light. Native peoples know leatherleaf as a powerful diuretic, to be used sparingly.

Once we trace ourselves into even a single thread of ecological connection, we feel a deep sense of country. Watch shadows of emaciated spruce tree sticks stripe your camper window. Feel beads of August rain, hear the scratches of wild night-music: Could you survive in the taiga?

Can you find them? . . . Dall sheep in Chitistone Gorge

A bee visits firewood

Or perhaps you are among the lucky few to visit coastal Wrangell-St. Elias. Listen to icebergs crackle in salt water, watch seals slide from icy perches into steel-gray waters. Imagine paddling hollowed cedar canoes down the churning Alsek River to the ocean as Tlingit traders often did. Don ornamental finery in respect to forces moving through Alsek waters. Above, precariously balanced chunks of ice dense enough to crush 10 canoes glint translucent blue. Offer a prayer and push into the Alsek current.

To feel the web of energy that is home, we must combine all ways of knowing. Limnologists and land-dwellers both know salmon distinguish family streams by smell and moon position. Elders and entymologists both know dark-winged butterflies absorb more light and pollinate more buds. They know these things in different mixes of experiment and experience. Together, traditional knowledge and scientific deduction may lead to a richer understanding of ecological lifestrands.

And richer understanding is needed. As is true all over earth, wasteful human consumption practices threaten the Bordercountry. No form of boundary protects lands, plants, and animals from global warming, and the thin margin of survival in the North makes Bordercountry life more vulnerable than ecosystems in more moderate climates. Human demand also endangers Bordercountry lifestrands: There are plans to clearcut coastal Malaspina rainforests.

Hiking, driving, or dreaming, we are all woven into the Bordercountry. These lands are yours to visit, to enjoy, and to protect. See them as sacred spaces, as parts of a whole none of us can afford to be without.

Eagle skull and dwarf fireweed

Mount Blackburn's summit disappears into a gray-black cloud. Lightning flashes and a low rumble of thunder reverberates off the massif. Fourteen thousand feet (4,267 m) below on Nugget Creek, the temperature drops and it begins to rain. The rain's intensity is tempered by its brevity. Within minutes a red, orange, and yellow rainbow appears, vivid against Blackburn's rocky ridgeline. Sunshine replaces rain, and the temperature soars back up to nearly 70 degrees F (21 degrees C). When the curtains of clouds lift from the surrounding peaks, sunlight glints off fresh snow. It is mid-June.

This is a land of extremes. From the ocean waters of the Gulf of Alaska to the glaciated peaks of the world's highest coastal mountain range, the region is diverse and awe inspiring. Six of North America's ten highest peaks, the largest piedmont glacier, wild rivers, boreal forests, and marsh wetlands combine to make this region's landscape unique. Shaping each landscape is the climate.

Climate is the principle architect of the immense mountain ranges and lake-dotted basins of the region. Climate determines whether an area has palm trees or sitka spruce, tundra or tropical forest, wolverine or boa constrictors. Landscaping tools include wind, water, heat, and cold. The Wrangell-St. Elias region spans three climatic zones: maritime, transitional, and continental. To better understand the weather within the area, let's take a climate tour. From Mount Blackburn we will visit the coast and finally the interior. On the way we will sample some typical June weather.

Mounts Blackburn and McCarthy and the Chitina River valley are in the transitional climatic zone. Lodged between the more temperate coastal zone and the climatic extremes of Alaska's interior, the lower elevations in the transition zone receive 10-24 inches (25-61 cm) of precipitation, far less than the coast but more than double that received in the interior. The area surrounding and including McCarthy provides a good example of a transitional climate. Located at the snout of the Kennicott Glacier, McCarthy experiences cold winters and warm summers. Temperatures range between -50 and 80 degrees F (-46 and 27 C). July is McCarthy's warmest month. McCarthy has more sunshine than the coast but less than the interior.

Less than 100 miles (161 km) to the south of Mount Blackburn, Prince William Sound is experiencing 55-degree F (13-degree C) temperatures and steady rain. A low-pressure storm system from the Aleutians is centered over the Gulf of Alaska, bringing rain to the lower elevations and snow to the peaks of the Chugach and St. Elias Mountains.

The combination of ocean and steep topography has created the largest assemblage of glaciers in North America. As moist maritime air masses climb over the

Storm over Nugget Creek

mountains, the air temperature drops, water vapor condenses, and it begins to rain or snow. Along the coast, mean annual precipitation exceeds 130 inches (330 centimeters). At higher elevations, much of the precipitation falls as snow. The 150-mile-long (241-kilometer-long) Bagley Ice Field and the 40-mile-wide (64-

kilometer-wide) Malaspina Glacier are products of average annual snowfalls of six hundred inches (fifty feet/fifteen meters). This abundance of snow builds and sustains the glaciers, many of which extend to sea level.

The Chugach and St. Elias mountains act as a dividing line for the maritime and transitional climatic zones. The mountain ranges are a massive barrier between the Pacific Ocean and the continental interior. The climatic effects are striking. At 2,600 feet (793 meters) the mountainside facing the Gulf of Alaska

receives twelve times the precipitation of the interior-facing slope.

The ocean is a moderating influence on coastal temperatures. Winter temperatures rarely drop below zero F (-18 C), and summer highs rarely rise above the lower 70s (about 22 C). Moderate temperatures and heavy precipitation characterize the maritime climate. Cloudy days far outnumber clear days. Clear weather is most likely to occur in early summer and in winter when high pressure systems reach the coast.

Approximately 100 miles (161 kilometers) to the north of Mount Blackburn in the village of Northway, Alaska, the skies are sunny and the temperature is 80 degrees F (27 degrees C). The last vestiges of winter are disappearing as summer solstice approaches. All the lakes on the Tetlin National Wildlife Refuge are ice-free, and the hills are vibrant green. On this June day, Northway has approximately nineteen hours of direct sunlight and plenty of light to take a midnight hike.

The communities of Haines Junction, Tok, Northway, and Glennallen share a continental climate, with temperature extremes varying by over 150 degrees F (66 degrees C). For example, record highs and lows for Northway are 91 and -72 degrees F (33 and -58 degrees C), a 163-degree F (91-degree C) difference. The temperatures reflect the extreme seasonal variations. Northway experiences 137 days a year when the mean temperature is below zero F (-18 C) and 34 days when the mean temperature is above 70 degrees F (21 degrees C). In winter, temperatures can plunge to -40 F (-40 C) for weeks at a time.

The interior is the sunbelt of the north, boasting more sunny days than either the coast or the McCarthy area. Northway receives approximately 9 inches (24 cm) of precipitation annually. Because of this, the continental climate is semiarid. Moisture stored in the snowpack and runoff from the mountains provide additional water during the growing season. Precipitation is greatest during the summer months.

The evening sun bathed the large, volcanic outcrop in warm reddish light. Picking up my camera, I began the climb to the turquoise pools on top of the lava domes. The calm green waters overlooking the silty turbulence of the Alsek River would be a perfect site for sunset pictures. As the sun slid toward the horizon, I scrambled up and down the gently undulating terrain toward my favorite pool. As I crested a ridge, I sensed I was not alone.

Twenty-five feet away stood a large grizzly bear. I could feel adrenaline surge as the bear and I stared at each other in surprise. Hackles raised, ears plastered against his head, the grizzly turned to face me. In what I hoped was a firm but friendly voice, I apologized for interrupting the bear's evening. Staring eye to eye, I waited for the charge. Hearing my voice seemed to mellow the bear. His ears returned to a more upright position. I began a slow retreat backward, carefully watching the bear. After a few tense moments, the grizzly appeared to relax. With additional distance between us, I decided to risk a picture. About the time the camera reached eye level, the bear decided that he also wanted a better look at me. Watching the grizzly take two steps in my direction focused my attention. Dropping my camera, I extended my arms above my head and told the bear the best lie I could think of: "You better watch out. I'm bigger than you." It worked. The bear's advance stopped, and he and I continued to retreat in opposite directions.

This was not my first bear encounter on the Alsek, nor would it be the last. It was, however, the closest. Too close for comfort. It is best to have a minimum of 150 feet (50 m) between you and a bear.

Grizzly bear

Over the course of the five day raft trip, we counted twenty-one bears. Boars, sows, cubs, and two-year-olds, black, brown, and blonde, bears of every sort and in a variety of groupings, including an odd pairing of a medium-sized black bear in proximity to a small grizzly with a distinctive blonde streak. Black bears usually avoid grizzly bears. Wild bears are solitary, traveling together only during mating season and when with cubs. Cubs usually stay with their mother for the first two to three years.

The Kluane area is estimated to have three to four hundred grizzly bears and approximately one hundred black bears. Kluane Park wardens are studying the grizzly bears, collecting information to assist the park in managing human use of grizzly bear habitat. Bears are especially abundant in the Alsek River Valley, where favored bear foods such as hedysarum roots, soapberries, and bearberries are found. They also like horsetails, plant roots, carrion, ground squirrels, salmon, and moose calves.

The area above the rock outcropping had a good crop of bearberries, while hedysarium roots were found in the vegetated areas along the banks of the Alsek. The bear probably came down to the pool for a drink of clear water.

The grizzly and I retreated to ridges a more comfortable 250 feet (76 m) apart. I snapped a picture and watched as the shaggy grizzly with big ears eyed me one final time. As he walked over the ridge, I thanked the bear. He had reacted with natural grace, allowing our close encounter a happy ending.

Map of the Bordercountry

Wrangell-St. Elias National Park
Kluane National Park Reserve
Tetlin National Wildlife Refuge

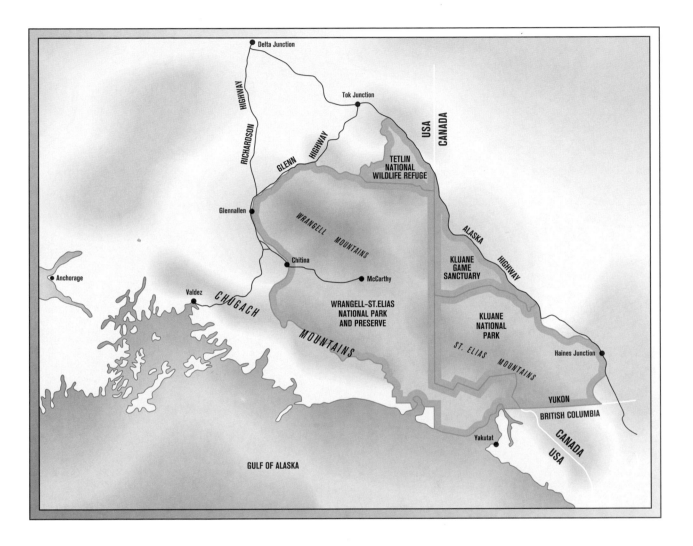

Kluane Lake reflections

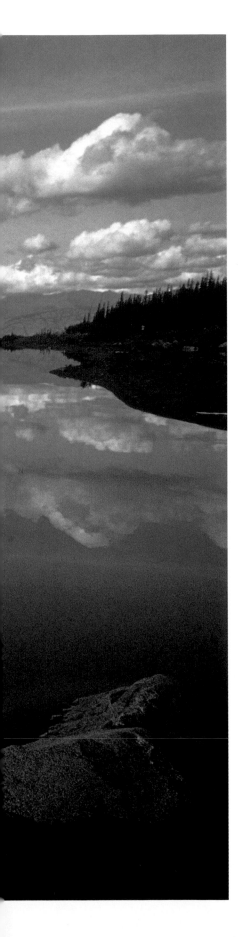

chapter four

KLUANE
NATIONAL
PARK RESERVE

A natural history book is worth its weight in glacial silt if it provides even one indispensable piece of information. Here is that essential tip: "Kluane" does *not* rhyme with "Duane." Canada's great national park of ice and rugged massifs is pronounced "kloo-WAH-nee" and means "place of many fish" in the language of the Native People of the region.

Whether driving from the United States or Canada, you will know you have arrived in big mountain country as you near Kluane National Park Reserve. Even if you get a sneak preview on a flight to Anchorage, we are certain your heart will thump in awe somewhere in these environs.

Multicolored mountains cut jagged lines across the sky, and glaciers of rock spill down to the highway. Lakes large enough to be called inland seas undulate silver-blue. In rare moments, valley openings reveal iced peaks dwarfing the 7,950 feet (2,500 m) mounts along the road. Do not drive by Kluane on your way to somewhere. Kluane National Park Reserve is as "somewhere" as you are ever likely to be.

Kluane National Park Reserve is a wonderful example of the difference between political and natural boundaries. Travelling between the Yukon and Alaska, you will pass through customs checkpoints. You may see a swath cut through surrounding spruce forests, which demarcates the international border. You will stop at official-looking buildings that confirm you are about to cross something of significance to humans.

A quick survey of the surrounding lands, however, provides little natural evidence of an important ecological boundary. You are neither crossing a watershed nor moving from lowlands to highlands. The border you cross has meaning only in the blink of an eye that nation-states named Canada and the United States will exist in earth time.

More obvious than the human lines is a wide, relatively flat area between the Kluane's rough-and-tumble Front Range mountains and the

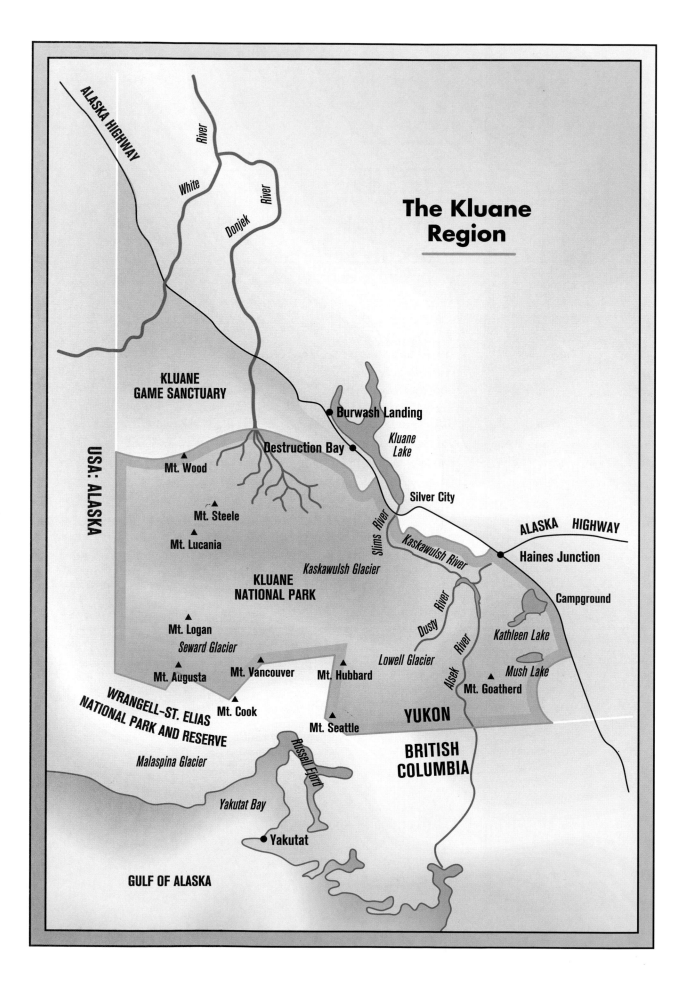

The Kluane Region

ALASKA HIGHWAY

White *River*

Donjek *River*

KLUANE GAME SANCTUARY

● Burwash Landing

Kluane Lake

Destruction Bay ●

▲ Mt. Wood

Silver City

Slims River

ALASKA HIGHWAY

▲ Mt. Steele

Kaskawulsh River

Haines Junction ●

▲ Mt. Lucania

Kaskawulsh Glacier

KLUANE NATIONAL PARK

Campground

Dusty River

Kathleen Lake

▲ Mt. Logan

Seward Glacier

Lowell Glacier

Alsek River

Mush Lake

▲ Mt. Augusta

▲ Mt. Vancouver

▲ Mt. Hubbard

▲ Mt. Goatherd

WRANGELL–ST. ELIAS NATIONAL PARK AND RESERVE

▲ Mt. Cook

YUKON

▲ Mt. Seattle

BRITISH COLUMBIA

Malaspina Glacier

Russell Fiord

Yakutat Bay

● Yakutat

GULF OF ALASKA

USA: ALASKA

rounded Ruby Range. Called the Shakwak Trench, this valley is part of the Denali fault line running northwest through interior Alaska. The Shakwak is visible from the point where the Haines Road crosses the Dezadeash River, then along Kluane Lake and the Alaska Highway 150 miles (241 km) to the northwest.

In geological terms, the Shakwak is a *graben*. Picture two blocks side by side, then imagine one of the blocks slipping vertically down. That is the Shakwak Valley.

Ruby Range rocks to the east are considerably older than the 12.5-million-year-old peaks of the St. Elias Range. Ice Age glaciers one million years ago widened and deepened the Shakwak Valley, but the landforms we see today were carved primarily in the last 25,000 years. The Shakwak portion of the Denali Fault is a segment of the conveyor belt moving Mount Logan ever so slowly westward over the Canada-U.S. political border.

Another natural boundary lies between the Front Ranges and the Kluane Icefields. Although road travelers see green lands edging the highway, more than half of the Kluane Park is layered with ice one mile (1.5 km) thick. A hike just 15 miles (24 km) from the Sheep Mountain Visitor's Centre to the face of the Kaskawulsh Glacier reveals how close the Icefields really are.

You may notice a difference in water color between the slate gray of the Slims River delta and the cobalt blue of Kluane Lake. The Slims River carries a tremendous amount of ground rock from the Kaskawulsh Glacier and dumps it in Kluane Lake waters. The Slims Delta is a boundary connecting ice and vegetation.

Behind the Front Ranges is the Duke Depression, a low valley separating the lower mountains from the high St. Elias peaks. The Duke River flows through the Depression, forming a geological border running southeast to northwest.

Mountains also create climatic boundaries. The south end of the park is influenced by maritime/coastal weather patterns, the north end by continental/interior weather. The maritime influence brings more precipitation to the southern portion of Kluane, translating into a greater variety of vegetation and a moderation of extreme temperatures.

Hikers in the north of the park joyfully discover an absence of alder thickets but may not know that colder mean temperatures and less precipitation are to thank for their bushwhacking reprieve.

Alder does not exist merely to impede human travel. Its roots "fix" atmospheric nitrogen in soil, enriching dirt for other plants. Absent nitrate-rich soil, some leafy creatures have difficulty photosynthesizing light into food and do not survive.

Sheep Mountain in the morning

Fewer plants, fewer animals. Moose, an ardent herbivore, favor the greater variety of greens in the south end of Kluane. They are a rarer sight in the northern park.

Nature's borders are neither straight nor fixed. In the middle of the Icefields, ice-free peaks pierce the vast glacial veil. Tiny tundra flowers bloom, pika scamper, and the occasional grizzly bear ambles. Called *nunataks*, these mountain tops are small islands pulsing with life in a great ocean of ice.

How did two-inch (5-cm) flowers and two-ounce (57-g) animals find their way across glacial seas? They may not have. One theory postulates that nunatak life predates the glaciers. When the ice rolled in, these plants and animals may have retreated to safe harbor in nunatak nooks and crannies. Nunataks may be the Bordercountry's Galapagos Islands.

Natural boundaries in the Bordercountry were very different before the mountains and ice started forming approximately 12.5 million years ago. Between sixty and twenty million years ago, the lands in the park area were gentle hills separated by broad valleys and clear rivers. The climate was probably much warmer than today: Imagine preparing for a tropical vacation in the Yukon.

Loud t-shirts and coconut oil may sound attractive, but consider that you might have had to avoid becoming lunch for large dinosaurs and been forced to outrun molten lavas from the Wrangell volcanos. Over time, the dinosaurs disappeared. Lush subtropical vegetation compressed into coal seams now visible near

Moon over Kluane

Amphitheatre Mountain. Look for volcanic material from the Wrangells along glacier-scoured rock walls in the Park interior.

Kluane lands probably originated to the south and rafted north on great plates of earth and ocean. Saint Elias massifs formed as rafting masses collided against the continent, creating ripples over 10,000 feet (3,048 m) high. Some of the rocks atop St. Elias peaks probably formed beneath the seas of the South Pacific. Others are closely related to formations in modern-day British Columbia and Washington state.

Perhaps ten million years ago temperatures dropped, and carpets of ice began to cover Kluane peaks and valleys. Ice-free areas at glacier edges were a wealth of nutrient-rich plants. Cool weather and nourishing food encouraged animal development.

A grizzly sow with her two cubs

Icebergs from the Lowell Glacier
floating in the Alsek River

And animals certainly did develop. Bears weighing 800 pounds (363 kg) may sound worthy of respect, but would you hike in a park boasting saber-toothed tigers, rhinoceroses, and wooly mammoth? These large mammals roamed ice-free lands at glacier edges tens of thousands of years ago. Some of the animals ranging through Kluane National Park Reserve today, including caribou, moose, and grizzly, first appeared during a time when beaver were as large as bear and cats had fangs.

Although natural distinctions between water and land may appear obvious, even lakes and rivers change line. Approximately twelve thousand years ago glaciers dammed the Alsek River valley, forming Recent Lake Alsek. Haines Junction and the Kathleen and Dezadeash River valleys were under water for thousands of years. Remnant benches of Lake Alsek are visible near Haines Junction and along the Alsek trail just north of Haines Junction. The glacial lake left a legacy of soil rich enough to support an experimental agricultural station, now used as the Kluane Park Headquarters.

Glacier-dammed lakes are not ancient history in Kluane. The Lowell Glacier has repeatedly dammed the Alsek River to create Recent Lake Alsek. Duplicating a pattern developed over thousands of years, the Lowell Glacier cut off the Alsek River in A.D. 1725 and broke in A.D. 1850 to create a lake flooding the Alsek, Kaskawulsh, and Dezadeash River valleys. When the ice dam broke, waters of Recent Lake Alsek inundated surrounding valleys and destroyed several coastal Indian villages. The Lowell Glacier may again dam the Alsek someday.

While crossing the highway bridge spanning the Slims River, give a thought to the lengthy travels of the glacier gray waters. They will flow 1,500 miles (2,400 km) northwest to the Bering Sea via the Yukon River. Given that the Gulf of Alaska in the Pacific Ocean is only 150 miles (240 km) away, the Slims River drainage route appears, well, slightly inefficient. What could Mother Nature have been thinking?

As is common in the Bordercountry, ice is the answer. One thousand years ago Kluane Lake drained south through the Slims, Kaskawulsh, and Alsek Rivers to the Gulf of Alaska. The Kaskawulsh Glacier advanced approximately five hundred years ago, blocking southward drainage and raising the level of Kluane Lake. Waters gradually cut a channel through hills at the lake's northern end, carving a route north to the Yukon River and the Bering Sea. Geologists predict that as the Kaskawulsh Glacier recedes, Kluane Lake may again drain south to the Gulf of Alaska.

Natural boundaries are a reflection of both present and past environmental changes. Current conditions influence vegetation distribution, but former Ice Age climates have left a mark. Some plants in the Kluane area are at their southern limit, others are at their northern maximum.

Around Shepard's Knoll, a short hike from the Sheep Mountain Visitor's Centre, you may catch a scent evoking ancient metamemories. Drop to the earth if you can, and smell the small green plants. They are *Artemisia rupestris*, a rare sage from the Eurasian plains of present-day Siberia. This plant may have travelled across the Bering land bridge from lands ancestral to many of us. Please respect these leafy travellers and do not pick them. Leave the sage to flourish and offer others a whiff of the Ice Ages.

Kokanee, a unique form of formerly land-locked sockeye salmon, are another reminder of glacial influences. These fish live in the connected waters of Kathleen, Louise, and Sockeye lakes (and in Fredrick Lake outside the park).

Adult salmon usually live in the ocean and return to the fresh waters of their birthplaces to spawn. Kokanee salmon, biologically indistinguishable from their sea-faring cousins, never leave the Kathleen Lakes system. Limnologists (fish scientists to the rest of us) speculate that salmon became stuck in fresh waters when the Lowell Glacier blocked the Alsek River to create Recent Lake Alsek. Although Lowell ice is not presently blocking Alsek waters, Kokanee have not resumed their

A grizzly with its fresh salmon catch

journey to the Gulf of Alaska. Who can blame them? It is, after all, a long and hazardous trip.

Kluane landforms influence river flow, lake depth, plant distribution, and animal movement. Imagine travelling along Kluane's sheer drops and tumbled boulder paths. Is it any wonder the animals of greatest number in Kluane National Park are Dall sheep and mountain goats?

Dall sheep ewes weigh 100 pounds (45 kg), and rams may tip the scales at 250 pounds (113 kg). Slightly smaller than their Bighorn relatives to the south, Dall sheep move with the change of season: up grassy mountain meadows in the summer and down to warm southern exposures in the winter. Your best chance to see Dall sheep from lower elevations is (of course) around the Sheep Mountain Visitor's Centre.

Approximately seven to eight hundred mountain goats live in the park, congregating around Goatherd Mountain and the Alsek Ranges. Kluane goats and sheep resemble each other from a distance, but goats have longer coats and hairy "leggings." Goats fare better in deep drifts and have displaced Kluane sheep in areas exposed to significant winter snowfalls.

Bear. The very word conjures contrasting images of cuddly toys and gaping jaws. Humans have a complex relationship with bears. These animals behave in ways we recognize as curiosity, dignity, power. Bears sit on their hind ends and pull at berry bushes with their front paws. Cubs tumble about their investigations in the same way human babies grasp shiny baubles. Adults saunter with an assurance of strength. They remind us of . . . ourselves.

Both black and brown (or grizzly) bear roam Kluane National Park. Although the common names distinguish the two bear species by color, black bears range from black to cinnamon, and grizzlies may be white-blonde to deep brown.

Smaller than brown bears and initially more timid, black bear tend to stick to areas of dense vegetation cover. If a grizzly is in the area, a black bear usually will move on. In Kluane, black bears are most often seen in the southeast area of the park and around the Kathleen Lake campground. Both brown and black bear may become "garbage bears" habituated to human food. Bears seeking human leftovers often end up shot as "problem" bears, but if it was your garbage the bear sought, the real "problem" is you. Keep a clean camp and your conscience guilt-free.

Grizzly bears have one of North America's last havens in Kluane National Park Reserve. Perhaps 250-400 brown bear live in Kluane, claiming areas of 5.8-11.6 square miles (15-30 sq km) each. Kluane's densest grizzly population is in the Slims River valley. As with all successful Bordercountry mammals, the grizzly bows to climate. Bears den between October and April and follow grasses, roots, and berries up and down valleys and slopes from spring to fall.

Ewes foraging with lambs

The Southern Tutchone Athabaskan people of the Kluane region valued the same plants and berries prized by grizzly bears. So would you if this country were your territory. As principal food gatherers, women were often in bear areas. The women travelled in groups and would yell before entering berry patches: "Be sorry for me, brother, I'm just around for berries like you."[1] As a sign of respect, the People also were careful to avoid stepping in bear scat or tracks.

Hikers today would do well to follow the ways of the Southern Tutchone: Watch for bear signs and make noise in bear country. Above all, respect these wild creatures who are connected to humans through myths and memories deep inside all of us.

[1] *From Trail to Highway: A guide to the places and people of the Southwest Yukon and Alaska Panhandle, the Champagne-Aishihik Band (Victoria, B.C. 1988).*

One of nature's great mysteries is how an animal can come to weigh 1,600 pounds (726 kg) on a diet of aquatic vegetation, willow, alder, and highbush cranberries. Ask the Bordercountry moose. Kluane moose are among the largest hooved animals on the planet and are fond of the cuisine around Kathleen Lake.

If you are very, very lucky, you may hear wolves sing across a moonlit spring Kluane evening. Several packs roam the park summer and winter. Kluane wolves play an important role in ecosystem equilibriums. Should you ever see a streak of gray running along a ridge or feel a deep howl along your spine, you too will know wolves as part of the balance of life.

Caribou are as characteristic of wild places as grizzly bear and wolves. Two resident herds of woodland caribou live near park boundaries and occasionally pound hooves across the Alaska Highway near the north end of Kluane Lake.

Large mammal encounters are a great thrill, a "Why-didn't-I-have-my-camera-ready" moment. But do not ignore the medium-to-small furry types. Arctic ground squirrel, pika, marmot, beaver, lynx, coyote, red fox, and snowshoe hare scamper, swim, whistle, jump, and lope throughout the park area. Pawprints of these critters are sure to be in your Bordercountry memories.

Get out of your car or motorhome at Kluane's self-guided rock glacier trail. The trail runs up a graded path to a sitting bench fifteen minutes from the highway. Signs along the trail (not wheelchair accessible) explain glacial formations under your feet and the expanse of country in front of you. The rocks you walk over are mountain scraps that travelled to this place in a sheet of ice taller than a skyscraper.

Cock an ear for the high whistle of the pika. Smell the wind. Watch rustles of alder up the hill, for a bear may be passing through. Do not hurry: The longer you stay, the more the country will reveal itself.

Ancient campsites north of the Bordercountry area of Kluane, Wrangell-St. Elias, and Tetlin indicate that people lived in the north Yukon at least twenty-five thousand years ago. That area was part of the ice-free corridor linking Asia and North America during the Ice Ages.

Evidence of human travel through the Bordercountry twenty-five thousand years ago probably has been ground to rock dust under glacial ice. Archaeologists have found spear points and bone tools suggesting an eight-thousand-year-old hunting camp near the Alaska Highway between Haines Junction and Whitehorse. Signs of other hunting camps of similar age have been found around the Brooks Arm of Kluane Lake and in the Danjak Valley.

The Old Ones lived on the land's terms: gathering, hunting, fishing, trapping, and travelling with the seasons. Groups of men and women hunted bison,

Evening in Kluane National Park

moose, and caribou on grassy lands sprouting from the rich soil legacy of Glacial Lake Champagne. Incomprehensible as it may seem, the people of Kluane hunted animals ten times their weight with nothing more than obsidian spear points. Bows and arrows were cultural developments that would not debut for thousands of years.

Archaeological finds aid in marking cultural shifts. Around 4,500 years ago the artifacts changed. Technological innovations were significant: People began notching obsidian blades to tie into spears. Humans had an obvious motivation to develop implements creating distance between themselves and 1,000-pound (454-kg) animals. Perhaps these tools contributed to human self-concepts of separation from other animals.

Over several thousand years the climate changed from temperate breezes to winds blowing glacier crystals. Humans also changed. Cultures came and went, and ancestors of the Southern Tutchone developed skills to live in the colder North. The People gathered roots, shoots, bark, and berries. Brush lean-tos around Klukshu and other meeting places served as summer homes during fishing time. In colder weather, the People retired to more permanent havens after hunting and trapping.

Many continue to depend on the land for food and medicine. A brief stop at Klukshu in the summer will convince you that fishing is no mere sport in this area.

Interior Southern Tutchone and the coastal Chilkat and Chilkoot Tlingit tribes had a brisk trade before Russians ever set foot in the "New World." The people of Kluane had furs, copper, and a lichen producing a yellow dye important in Chilkat weaving. Tlingits had cedar and euchalon, a fish that burns like oil when dried.

The Tlingit, known to be fierce, were none too keen on sharing their lucrative trading routes with Europeans. For many years, the Tlingit operated as daunting middlemen between Russians and Euro-americans, and interior Athabaskans.

Metal traps, guns, metal cookware. Imagine the changes such tools fostered. What would it mean to suddenly be able to cook in a pot directly over the fire instead of spending hours adding heated rocks to bark containers to boil water?

The Tlingit monopoly did not last. Jack Dalton was one of the first white men to journey to interior Yukon. In 1890, Dalton reached Nesketaheen, a center of Tlingit-Tutchone commerce, then returned to the coast via the Alsek River. The next year he returned to Nesketaheen with horses, another Interior first. With Native guides from the north, Dalton travelled inland as far as Kluane Lake.

Over the next few years Dalton established a trail and trading posts along the traditional Chilkat valley route. Those driving the road to Haines, Alaska, follow part of the Chilkat trail.

In the 1890s, gold shone brighter in the Yukon than anywhere else in the world. The Klondike Yukon was the place to be for the adventurous and the ambitious. Many of the sixty thousand-plus who journeyed to the goldfields paid Jack Dalton $2.50 per horse (a small fortune in those days) to travel over "his" trail and bunk in his roadhouses.

By 1903, lands around the Sheep Mountain Visitor's Centre were under *stampede*. Read a map and you will know where things looked promising: Bullion Creek, Silver City. On the southeast side of Kluane Lake, Silver City boasted a post office, cabins, and an outpost of the Canadian Northwest Mounted Police. Now nothing more than log ruins, the boom towns are a reminder of the fleeting value of mineral wealth.

Between Gold Rush days and the Second World War, Kluane was relatively quiet. The Jacquot brothers of Burwash Landing offered trophy-hunting experiences luxurious enough to lure United States senators, and mountaineers sought to stand atop St. Elias peaks. Canadian-U.S. boundary surveyors skied glaciers and measured mountains to set the international boundary. But thousands of desperate miners were gone. For people calling this place home, life again had a deeper rhythm.

Then came World War II, and the Bordercountry took on a new role as strategic military lands. International fears that Japan would attack and invade North America from the Pacific materialized as the 1,616-mile (2,600-kilometer) Alaska Highway.

Political fear is a strong motivator. In just nine short months, U.S. Army personnel blasted, shoveled, and slogged through the lands out the window of your camper. Mosquitos bit in summer and winds bit in winter. Army personnel, many of whom were African-Americans segregated from overseas duty, dug the Alaska Highway from rock wall, soggy tundra, and ice-cold rivers. In nine months, World War II birthed twentieth century Yukon and Alaska.

Half a century later, most Bordercountry visitors come in search of peace. We dream of seeing a glacier or a grizzly. We hope for nothing more than gentle weather and a good campsite.

Visiting the Park

First stop: Kluane National Park Visitor's Centre in Haines Junction. Southern Tutchone called the area Dakwakada ("High Cache"); Haines Junction has been a central meeting point for many generations. The site was a convenient place to fish for salmon before glaciers blocked access to the Gulf of Alaska and was near major Native trading routes to the coast and the interior.

Kluane Visitor's Centre is a friendly place with maps, information, interpretative displays, and slide shows. For the geologically-minded, the Visitor's Centre has a seismograph monitoring earth tremors in the area. Things may look solid to you, but the Visitor's Centre seismograph records an average of three earthquakes per day.

Strategically located across from the Visitor's Centre is a wonderful bakery. Motels, RV campgrounds, hot showers, and a general store/post office/bank are also in Haines Junction. True art lovers should not miss a close encounter with the "Animal Muffin," an interesting work of sculpture at the junction of Haines Road and the Alaska Highway.

Kluane National Park visitors range from the on-my-way-to-Denali crowd to weekend campers to scientists, trekkers, and mountain climbers. Park lands hold something for everyone, but remember that once off the highway, these lands are wild and remote. Plan your visit to match your outdoor experience and comfort levels.

Kathleen Lake is a convenient center for explorations in the south area of the park. The interpretive rock glacier trail is a fifteen-minute drive south of the lake. Kathleen Lake campground is spacious and includes disabled camper sites and an indoor kitchen.

Kathleen Lake day activities include fishing, hiking, and boating. Be cautious with Kathleen Lake: These waters can change from enticing jewel to windy nightmare in minutes.

The Haines Road World Heritage Site north of the campground offers a clear view of Kathleen and a reminder of the uniqueness of the Bordercountry. In 1979 Kluane National Park Reserve and the Wrangell-St. Elias National Park became the first international United Nations World Heritage Site. The designation means that all the world recognizes the importance of protecting these lands. In 1992 Glacier Bay National Park in Alaska was added to the World Heritage Site, and in 1993 a new British Columbia provincial park gave protection to part of the Tatenshini River watershed. These refuges may someday be consolidated into the largest internatinal World Heritage Site on earth.

Backcountry explorations in the south area of the park are limited only by your experience. The St. Elias Lake Trail is a gentle 2.5-mile (4-km) grade up approximately 492 feet (150 m). The trail to King's Throne rises 3,937 feet (1,200 m) in 3.1 miles (5 km) and involves snow, steeps, and stiff winds. Either will give you a feel for the land.

In summer and winter, the Cottonwood Trail from Kathleen and Louise lakes around Mush and Bates lakes and back to the highway is a fine adventure. Kathleen Lake owes its clarity to the deep delta at the base of Victoria Creek. The delta divided a single glacial-carved lake into Louise and Kathleen, leaving the gray glacial silt in Louise and flooding Kathleen with cobalt-bright waters.

Near Haines Junction, the Auriol Trail and Alsek River Trail are two backcountry favorites. The Auriol Trail climbs 4,265 feet (1,300 m) in seven miles (11 km) and offers an overview of the Front Ranges and the Shakwak Valley. The Alsek River Trail can be a day hike or a multiday trip (35 miles/56 km roundtrip with a gain of 131 feet/40 m). Look for tell-tale signs of Recent Lake Alsek benches along the cliffs above.

Kluane Park Visitor's Centre

Along the Auriol Trail

The Slims River valley is the most frequently hiked area in the park. From a stroll to Shepard's Knoll to a multiday trip up Observation Peak or over the Sheep-Bullion Plateau, exploration possibilities are numerous.

Check in at the Sheep Mountain Information Centre for suggestions and trail information. You must register with park staff at the information centre before any backcountry trip. To discourage bear encounters, Kluane Park rules require that backpackers use food canisters on any Slims River area overnight trip.

Just outside the park on the southeast shore of Kluane Lake are the remains of Silver City, the local goldrush town. Try as hard as you can to resist feeding the furry critters living in abandoned buildings.

Before leaving the Sheep Mountain area, stop at Soldier's Summit along the Highway. On a stormy day in November, 1942, Ottawa Member of Parliament Ian MacKenzie and Alaska U.S. Senator-to-be Bartlett cut a ribbon to officially open the Alaska Highway. The site is now a park exhibit.

The Yukon Territorial Government maintains a campground at Congdon Creek (named after a turn-of-the-century local politico) north of Sheep Mountain. The campground is a convenient base for north Kluane adventures. As in the south end of the park, adventures are limited only by your time and back-country experience.

The north end of the park is the Donjek/Duke Depression access. Amphitheatre Mountain, a three-to-four-day hike in the north area leads through tundra flower fields to a glacial cirque where coal ribbons wrap mountains in twenty-million-year-old fossilized leaves. Wrangell lavas from twenty-five million years ago color Amphitheatre a deep earth-red.

Hiking into the remote north park is for well-traveled backcountry trekkers only. Again, be sure to register with park staff for any overnight trips.

A few have the time and experience to travel the Icefield and ascend some of the largest peaks in North America. A few more can hike for days into the wild green valleys and mountains of the Front Ranges or raft Kluane rivers. Even a few more will leave their cars and walk the self-guided Rock Glacier Trail, stop at the Sheep Mountain Visitor's Centre, or join an interpretive hike. Be one of those people. Kluane will leave you with a deep understanding of the true meaning of "boundary."

The toughest part of any winter camping trip is separating yourself from the cozy warmth of your sleeping bag. This morning we are up early, drawn out by the promise of an exceptional day. The evening alpenglow has been replaced by a rosy dawn. Pudding and Dalton passes lie before us. Gliding through the white spruce into a forest of aspen, we discuss the advantages of winter camping: no bugs, tussocks, or wild river crossings, fewer people, and greater visibility.

In winter a new world awaits. As if opening a venetian blind to the natural world, winter provides nature lovers with an unobscured view. Gone are the green grass and leaves of deciduous shrubs and trees. The winter landscape highlights the vastness of the land while revealing intimate details of the land's inhabitants.

Animals' daily lives are reflected in the snow. Tracks tell many stories. Our tracks would tell the story of four skiers pulling sleds, slowly gaining elevation, climbing up the rolling terrain of Pudding Pass.

We are skiing the Cottonwood Trail. A favorite Kluane National Park summer hike, the trail runs from Kathleen Lake, along Cottonwood Creek, over Pudding and Dalton passes to Alder Creek in the Mush and Bates lakes drainages. Every March, Kluane park wardens snowmobile-pack an 53-mile (85-km) ski trail on the Cottonwood loop.

From the tracks we observe the trail is used more frequently by four-legged creatures than the two-legged variety. Lynx, moose, and a wolf pack share the trail

Climbing the Cottonwood Trail

Cottonwood Trail

with my companions and me. We estimate that the wolf pack whose tracks we are following has four to five members. The tracks are fresh, clearly outlined in two inches (5 cm) of newly fallen snow. The wolves trot from side to side on the trail, sometimes in single file, sometimes two abreast.

For over two miles (3 km) we follow the tracks, guessing the makeup of the pack. As I round each bend, I hope to see the wolves. To our disappointment, our four-day ski trip ends without a sighting. Just following the tracks, however, adds excitement to an already wonderful trip.

By mid-March the Yukon is thawing out from a long cold winter. Spring temperatures vary from -10 degrees F to nearly 50 degrees F (-23 degrees C to 10 degrees C) in the midday sun. The alpenglow at sunrise and sunset casts a softness to the starkly beautiful landscape, highlighting ridgeline cornices, making mountainsides come alive in patterns of shadow and light.

Although the trail crosses two passes, the terrain is gentle and varied. From the mountain-edged Kathleen Lake, the trail opens into the broad Alsek River valley and then climbs the first of two passes. Pudding Pass is gently rolling, whereas Dalton Pass is more of a climb. The Mush Lake side of Dalton Pass offers some easy telemark skiing terrain. The most challenging portion of the trip is the final descent through the trees beneath Dalton Pass to Alder Creek.

This trip is suitable for intermediate to advanced skiers who have winter camping and wilderness travel skills. Sections of the trail (for example, the mountainside after Kathleen Lake and Dalton Pass) run beneath potential avalanche chutes, so skiers need to be aware of

Winter camping

avalanche conditions and have the experience necessary to select a safe route.

The Cottonwood Trail is one of eight trails Kluane Park has identified for winter recreation. The other trails run in length from .9 to 13 miles (1.5 to 21 km). Some of the trails are groomed for classical and skate skiing. A winter recreation guide is available from the park.

Tetlin National Wildlife Refuge

chapter five

TETLIN
NATIONAL
WILDLIFE REFUGE

Tetlin National Wildlife Refuge is a place of quiet beauty: broad muskeg, oxbow lakes, rounded hills. These lands are as wonderous as the heights of Kluane and the rocky coasts of Wrangell-St. Elias. The Refuge nurtures life both resident and transient: its peat-filled wetlands are home to wolf and bear, and host to migrating sandhill cranes.

Tetlin is a point on the migration map for caribou and migratory waterfowl and for humans travelling the Alaska Highway. Many travellers of the featherless biped variety make the mistake of passing along the edge of the refuge without stopping for a closer look at this million-acre sanctuary. Do not miss the opportunity to learn more about one of the most important migratory crossroads in North America.

The triangular Tetlin Refuge borders Wrangell-St. Elias National Park to the south and the Yukon Territory to the southeast. Most of the northeastern boundary of the refuge parallels the Alaska Highway. Rising from broad river basins to the foothills of the craggy Mentasta-Nutzotin mountains, the Tetlin Refuge supports many northern lifewebs.

Although small in comparison to Wrangell-St. Elias and Kluane national parks, the refuge is home to approximately fifty species of mammals, including moose, caribou, Dall sheep, grizzly and black bear, wolves, wolverine, lynx, red fox, otter, beaver, and snowshoe hare. Freshwater lakes and streams support arctic grayling, burbot, lake trout, northern pike, and whitefish.

Tetlin is of critical importance to migratory waterfowl. Almost 150 kinds of birds nest on the refuge, and another 60-odd species rest here on their way north or south. As many as one hundred thousand ducklings are born in a Tetlin spring. Imagine all those young ducks learning how to handle the skies before winter winds start to blow—an air traffic controller's worst nightmare.

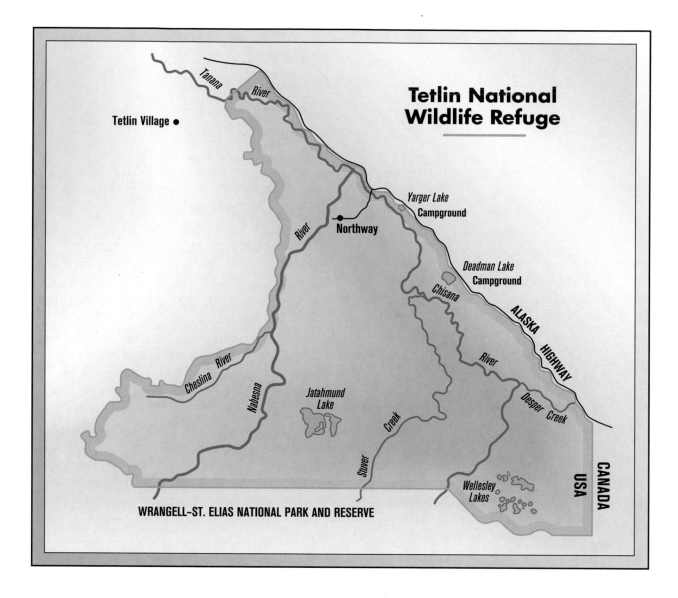

Each spring and fall, the silence of the refuge is broken by the sounds of two hundred thousand migrating lesser sandhill cranes, tundra swans, lesser Canadian geese, and a cacophony of other species. Trumpeter swan pairs curve their willowy necks over the waters of Tetlin Refuge lakes.

Perhaps you stop for a short hike at Tetlin's Yarger Lake along the edge of the Alaska Highway. You watch a pair of swans move across the lake with the grace of Russian ballet stars. Although you try not to disturb their quiet dance, you startle them. The birds labor to lift heavy wings, initiating an arduous transition from water to air. Issuing a sonorous trumpet, the swans rise upward. Their great wings move with an audible "whoosh, whoosh." And now you feel the magic of the Tetlin Refuge.

Birds of prey also favor the Tetlin Refuge. Tetlin and surrounding lands host the largest nesting concentration of ospreys in Alaska. For those who have never seen the national bird of the United States, you may well get your chance in the

Bordercountry. Bald eagle nests are common along Tetlin rivers and lakes.

A soaring bald eagle with wings spread wide as the sun is a thrilling sight. Should you arrange for an airplane ride into the public use cabin at Tetlin's Jatahmund Lake, you might see how smaller animals and birds react to the appearance of the flying predator.

Watch as two young loons paddle after their parents in jerked strokes, emitting unrefined calls resembling the turn of rusty gears. At lake's edge a black spruce sways with the weight of a bald eagle. Hooded eagle eyes follow the young family, watching, waiting.

Sensing danger, the parents set off wailing, bone-chilling sirens. The eagle moves into the sky, soaring close to the loon chicks. He folds his wings in a swoop, diving to catch a young one in his talons. The adult loons raise upper bodies from the lake surface; water sprays from their flapping wings. Confused, the eagle misses his target. The great predator flies off, his talons grasp only air. There is no good and evil here—merely the raw edge of life and death.

Tetlin Refuge is a place of migration. Over time, plants, animals, birds, and humans have passed through these lands. Now you too travel the Tetlin Bordercountry.

As you follow your own migratory route, take a moment to acknowledge those who have gone before. During the great Ice Ages, thousands of humans and other animals travelled across the Bering Strait land bridge and through the ice-free corridor just to the north of the refuge.

Artifacts found in the Yukon Territory indicate that people were near the Bordercountry twenty-seven thousand years ago. One hundred miles (161 km) to the north, near Healy Lake, Alaska, archaeologists have uncovered a village at least eleven thousand years old. Camps of the Old Ones have also been identified near refuge lakes and rivers.

Today you may see the soft grays and browns of woodland caribou, but twenty thousand years ago saber-toothed tigers, wooly mammoth, and bison roamed Bordercountry grasslands. Hungry people followed the animals. Some stayed in the North and some continued their migration, eventually settling in the southwestern United States.

The First People of Tetlin are known as Dene Athabaskans. Linguistic relationships among groups of the Dene, from the Upper Tanana River valley

Common loon

Athabaskans to the Navajo and Apache in the southwestern United States, attest to the long tradition of migration through the Tanana Basin and Tetlin Refuge area.

Traditionally, the Upper Tanana Athabaskans of the Tetlin area lived according to the rhythms of the land: hunting and gathering with seasonal cycles of plants and animals. Life was busy in the spring, summer, and fall with fishing and trapping. Winters were meditative times of sewing, trapping, beading, and storytelling.

The People had semipermanent homes in the winter and summer camps near reliable fishing grounds. In good years, caribou, sheep, moose, snowshoe hare, fish, waterfowl, and wild plants provided rich sustenance to those able to harvest the harsh abundance of the Tanana Valley. In lean years, the Tetlin area people survived the winter primarily on dried fish, meat, and plants stored for the hard times.

Upper Tanana peoples continue to depend on the land for food and cultural identity today. For Native peoples, subsistence living is a way of life dependent on nature rather than monetary wages; it is not just a form of food gathering. "Subsistence" is now spelled with a capital "S" and is viewed by Native elders as one of the few ways left to pass traditional cultural values on to young people. Subsistence foods are still a central focus of family and village ceremonies.

In 1991 the village of Northway, an Athabaskan community predating the refuge, hosted an important potlatch to celebrate the 115th birthday of Chief Walter Northway. Imagine the changes Chief Northway had witnessed since the day in the early 1900s when he and his father aided two lost and hungry white men, the first the young Northway had ever seen.

Although the Athabaskans of the Upper Tanana Valley began trading with the British and the Russians in the 1840s, few Europeans trekked refuge lands. Several government-sponsored reconnaissance trips did float rivers of the future refuge during the next sixty years, including Lieutenant Henry Allen's remarkable expedition up the north Tanana River to the Yukon.

The quiet movement of the North changed forever when news of gold spread to the South in the 1890s. A strike in 1913 in the Chisana River headwaters (now in the Wrangell-St. Elias National Park) turned the Tanana River and Refuge area into a bustling travelway. Steamboats chugged commerce up the Tanana, and lands now home to bog rosemary boasted busy trading posts.

For most of those who rushed to Chisana, the rumor of boom became a reality of bust. Claims, cabins, and trading posts were abandoned. The steamboats stopped smoking. The Bordercountry settled back into slower land rhythms.

World War II yanked the Bordercountry into the twentieth century. As part of the joint Canadian-American defense against the Japanese, the United States Army Air Corps constructed a runway in Northway. The strip became one of the airbases comprising a strategic air supply route stretching from western Canada through Alaska. The 1941 building of the Alaska Highway, completed in just nine months, ensured that the Tetlin area would not fall quiet again.

Visiting the Refuge

As you travel the Alaska Highway along the refuge boundary or explore the lands of Tetlin, trace migration routes of countless plants, animals, and humans. For most of earth time, Bordercountry life has moved with weather and availability of food.

Tetlin Refuge sign

(next page) Moonrise over Tetlin National Wildlife Refuge

Today humans travel north for pleasure and have the luxury of the Tetlin National Wildlife Refuge Visitor Center to guide their way. Take a break from the road and stop at the inviting log cabin visitor center on your drive between Canada and Alaska. Stretch your legs on the ballroom-sized deck overlooking the Scotty and Desper Creek basins, and enjoy the view of the Black Hills and the snow-capped Nutzotins. These rounded slopes are leftovers from the farthest reach of the Wrangell glaciers.

The Tetlin Visitor Center is constructed of century-old white spruce harvested from the site of an interior Alaska fire. A husband-and-wife team hand-peeled all the logs in less than two weeks, then, with a crew, cut each log to fit tightly over the one below. To appreciate the skill of the builders, try slipping a credit card between two of the logs—even the fierce Tanana Valley winter winds cannot breathe through.

The picturesque visitors' center sod roof is authentic but not very practical—because sod retains moisture. The roof is an example of pioneer insulation. The extra warmth comes at a price: A roof the size of this one can soak up enough precipitation to place an extra 50,000 pounds (22,680 kg) of stress on the structure.

Several interpretive displays in the visitors' center will help you get a feel for refuge animals. Feel the stiff guard hairs of a black bear and the softness of lynx fur. Compare the size of your prints to those of a grizzly and a wolf. Do you suddenly feel small and vulnerable?

Visitors' center rangers present interpretive talks throughout the summer about the refuge and can provide information on other Alaska National Wildlife Refuges. Books and other materials are available for purchase.

A desire to understand the interconnected web of life is important to an appreciation for the Tetlin Refuge. You must be willing to look away from big mammals and big mountains.

When we hear the word "wilderness," most of us envision animals: a stream of caribou or the sable-brown ruff around a grizzly bear. But plants, too, have their drama. The colors of fall leaves, the lean of angular black spruce, and the bloom of Alaska cotton grass tell a story of the land.

Bald eagle

Because Bordercountry bog cannot cycle adequate nitrogen and phosphorous through the soil for photosynthesis, some plants have taken a liking to meat. The sundew, Alaska's version of the Venus fly trap, ensnares unwary insects in sticky oozing fluids.

Where there are sundew plants, there are muskeg, peat, and probably *permafrost*, or permanently frozen ground. Some ecologists believe bogs form from mature spruce communities, whereas others believe bogs precede the development of the spruce forests.

Black spruce with bad posture is another tip-off to permafrost. Because the ground is permanently frozen two feet (.6 m) or so under the surface, tree roots must grow long and shallow. The roots keep the tree fed but not fully upright. Just another concession to the harsh northern climate.

The smallest plants of the Tetlin wetlands and subalpine tundra are among the refuge's most arresting sights. Beneath your boots lie elfin groves of brilliant carnelians, deep maroons, blues, greens, and ochres—a carpet of Dr. Seuss forests.

Boreal forest and calm river

Those making an autumn drive along the refuge cannot help but remark on Mother Nature's talent for pointillism artwork. Golds, yellow-greens, and evergreens stipple the rolling lands in a confetti celebration of life before dormancy and death.

Nature's paintbrush is fire. Destructive as it may appear, natural fires actually enrich the lands with new plants and minerals. After a fire burns through an area, the first full-sized trees to stretch up are the deciduous poplar, birch, and quaking aspen. Where you see colors in the fall, you can be sure fire has passed through. Evergreen spruce trees may not reappear for one hundred years after a burn.

From Milepost 1305 to Tok, the scenery is a snapshot of a 1990 fire that burned over 90,000 acres (36,422 hectares). The fire forced evacuation of both Tetlin Village and Tok and closed the Alaska Highway. From fire comes renewal: Humans and animals alike feasted on a bumper crop of postfire morel mushrooms. The lands are regenerating. Magenta and green fireweed plants now display still-life summer fireworks in the burn area.

Lynx

Topography and vegetation create habitats, and animals move in. Tetlin Refuge hills, muskeg, and taiga forests are rich in wildlife. To maximize viewing opportunities, imagine yourself as a Bordercountry animal. Think of the foods you would eat and the landscape that offers protection. Timing is also important: Many animals are most active at dawn and during twilight. Above all, be patient. Pick a spot to sit and become part of the land.

Moose favor willows, shrubs, and aquatic plants; keep your eyes open near lakes and ponds. Grizzly bears tend to stay in the hilly area in the south of the refuge where plants and berries flourish. Wolf packs roam the refuge, usually far from human eyes, but you never know....

Snowshoe hares thrive on low willows and are most comfortable in the protection of black spruce and brush. Where there are bunnies, there are lynx. The flash of a tufted ear may be all you see, but even a blurred vision is enough to fill you with a sense of the Tetlin wilds. Look for beaver lodges on ponds near the highway: That SLAP! of a tail on the water is a sure sign the beaver has seen you, even if you cannot see her.

Waterfowl are visible on lakes and ponds throughout the refuge. Listen for the haunting tremolo of the Pacific loon at Deadman Lake. Among Tetlin's many water birds, the blue-winged teal, ring-necked duck, and lesser yellowlegs nest on the laced network of refuge waters. Dedicated birders can obtain checklists at the visitor center.

The Tetlin Refuge has erected nine interpretive exhibits along the Alaska highway. Each exhibit tells a story about the refuge area, from "The Land, The People" to "Highways of Water." An interpretive one-quarter-mile (1.2-km) walk near Deadman Lake identifies specific plants of the area and leads to a viewing deck on the edge of the lake. These exhibits will add to your appreciation of the refuge and taiga, or boreal forest, of interior Alaska. A 1.25 mile (2 km) walk along the trail to Hidden Lake (Mile 1240/Km 1996) provides a nice leg stretch and a quick taste of the refuge.

Fishing is a favorite Tetlin visitor activity. Burbot in the rivers, arctic grayling in Scotty and Desper creeks, and northern pike and whitefish in the lakes keep refuge fishing enthusiasts baiting their hooks.

Because the refuge is primarily taiga and water-logged muskeg, hiking is often a soggy venture. Boating—by paddle or motor—is probably the best way to see the the refuge. Desper Creek (Mile 1226.3/Km 1973.5) has a canoe launching area, and Deadman Lake (Mile 1249.4/Km 2010.7) has a boat ramp.

Experienced canoeists enjoy the multiple-day float trip from Desper Creek to near Northway; ask Visitor Center rangers for maps and details. For the casual paddler, Deadman and Yarger lakes offer a lazy Sunday afternoon every day of the week. As any boater knows, weather can change a quiet paddle into a serious situation, so be sure to stay aware of weather patterns before planning any trip.

For the seeker of sanctuary, the refuge offers two remote lake cabins available to the public. Accessible only by air, the cabins at Jatahmund Lake and Wellesley Lakes sleep six and are stocked with cooking gear. Visitors need to make reservations at the refuge office in Tok and must arrange for air taxi service.

When looking to pitch your tent or park your vehicle, try the refuge's Deadman Lake or Lakeview campgrounds. Deadman Lake (Mile 1249.3/Km 2010.5) is 1.5 miles (2.4 km) off the Alaska highway on an improved road. Each site has a fire ring and picnic table. There also is a disability-accesible public restroom. These first-come-first-served sites are short on amenities but are long on scenery and quiet. The eight Lakeview sites are similar to those at Deadman but are not suitable for large recreational vehicles because turnaround space is limited.

Other public campgrounds in the refuge area include the Tok River State Recreation Area and the Eagle Trail State Recreation Area, both located near Tok. The Tok River campground offers an interpretive trail accessible to those experiencing disabilities. Tok has several motels, private campgrounds, and RV villages. When in Tok, stop at the Tetlin Refuge headquarters across from the Alaska Public Lands Center for information on the refuge.

Tetlin National Wildlife Refuge is a resting place for migratory animals of all species. Including humans. There is much to see in this wetlands sanctuary. Do not pass it by.

Canoeing on Deadman Lake

There was a lonely beauty to the howl. It echoed in my dream, a sound alien yet known, out of place but distantly familiar. Was I dreaming? I drifted into consciousness, realizing the lone wolf's cry was real. Refuge Ranger Craig Perham stumbled to the cabin door. "He's right out front," Craig whispered. I slid out of my sleeping bag into the cold of the morning, one hand groping for my camera bag.

A solitary black wolf sat on the white ice of Jatahmund Lake in the middle of the Tetlin National Wildlife Refuge. He howled to the Mentasta and Nutzotin mountains, rosy in the early morning light. Scanning his surroundings, the wolf sat quietly for several minutes before standing, stretching, and loping off across the lake. Camera in hand, I followed to the lake shore, taking pictures as the wolf became a dot on the morning horizon.

Inside the cabin, biological technician Hank Timm fired up the stove and downed an aspirin. Timm was hurting. He was not the only one. Two days of bouncing up and down on a snowmobile had fried my leg muscles and curled my fingers. I consoled myself with the fact that even Hank, a former Alaska Wilderness Classic race winner, was feeling the effects of ten hours a day on the snow machines. For the last two days, we had covered over 70 miles (113 km) each day checking the Fish and Wildlife trapline.

Most trappers check their traplines every week or two, but they aren't trying to catch a live animal. Hank and Craig check the line each day, springing the traps if the temperature drops below -20 degrees F (-29 degrees C). This reduces the risk of hurting the animals. The

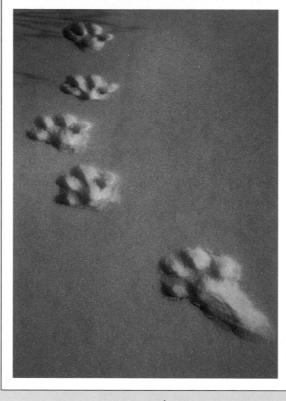

Lynx tracks

goal of the trapline is information, not pelts. Craig and Hank are collecting information on live lynx as part of a cooperative U.S. Fish and Wildlife, National Park Service, and Alaska State Fish and Game study. In the past year they have captured, weighed, aged, collared, and released 11 lynx. The information they learn gives the sponsoring agencies a more detailed picture of Alaska's only native cat.

The lynx is a medium-sized, short-tailed cat, similar to the bobcat but distinguished by its black-tipped tail, long legs, large furry feet, and elegantly tufted ears. Adult lynx weigh from 18-48 pounds (8-18 kg), with the males generally larger than the females. Their spotted gray fur is dense and warm, enabling lynx to weather the cold of the Alaskan interior.

So far this trapping season, only three lynx had been captured. Craig attributed the poor capture rate to the fact that this was mating season for the lynx. Not even fox urine or beaver scent were attracting the cats. Only the trail sets were successful. Placed in the middle of the trail, the sets use a leg snare that triggers when the animal steps into the loop and onto the release pad. The snare then tightens on the animal's leg. The snares that Fish and Wildlife use have "stops" that limit how tight the snare closes on the animal's leg.

Once caught, the animals are tranquilized and weighed; the biologists then pull a tooth to determine age and attach a radio collar. The animal is then released. For the lynx the experience is traumatic but temporary. It wakes up with a temporarily sore mouth and sports a radio collar. The collar does not seem to

A mirage at Jatahmund Lake

slow the lynx down. One of the big collared males was sighted on a fresh caribou kill the day after being captured and collared. With this study resource managers hope to develop a better understanding of lynx, their habits, prey, range, density, and population cycles.

The morning is half over before we are ready to go. A leisurely breakfast and a stubborn snowmobile make for a late departure. It will be well after dark before we return to the cabin. The slow start has one major benefit: The temperature has warmed to 7 degrees F (-14 degrees C). I watch for the wolf as we cross Jatahmund Lake.

Alpenglow on Mount Drum

chapter six

WRANGELL- ST. ELIAS
NATIONAL PARK

If ever there were a time to pop Edvard Grieg's *Peer Gynt Suite* into your tape deck, this is it. We recommend you skip straight to *In the Hall of the Mountain King*.

Wrangell-St. Elias National Park and Preserve, all 13,188,024 acres (5,337,030 hectares) of it, is a place where even a vocabulary steeped in superlatives is inadequate. Consider that 15 miles (24 km) from the ocean, Mount St. Elias reaches 18,008 feet (5,489 m) toward the sky. And that Malaspina Glacier is (as anyone who has read a word about this region knows) the size of the state of Rhode Island. Next door is the Bagley Icefield, part of North America's largest subpolar icefield. And that from the Wrangell volcanos flows one of the world's longest interior valley glaciers, the 75-mile (121-km) Nabesna. This land is big.

Mount Wrangell, an active volcano, is frosted with 250 square miles (64,750 hectares) of ice. Nine of the sixteen highest peaks of the United States rise from the lands of the park. More glacial silt muddies the waters of the Copper than any other river in the United States. The farthest inland reach of the Sitka spruce, the largest tree of the North, is in the park's Bremner Valley. Summers sweat 90 degrees F (32 degrees C) and winters chill to -70 degrees F (-57 degrees C). Humans do big things here, too: The Kennecott Mine produced the highest yield of copper of any lode in North America.

Gold mines, grizzly bears, permafrost, sand dunes, trumpeter swans, seals, hummingbirds, Ice Age vegetation, and some of the world's hungriest mosquitos: All are here in Wrangell-St. Elias National Park.

Most of us will never see Mount St. Elias, cross the Nabesna Glacier, or tussle with Bremner Valley alder. For all practical purposes, the greater part of the park is inaccessible. Just as well. These fenceless lands are among the last wild places on earth. Spaces large enough to accommodate Dall sheep and migrating caribou herds; roaring rivers and still ponds reflecting

119

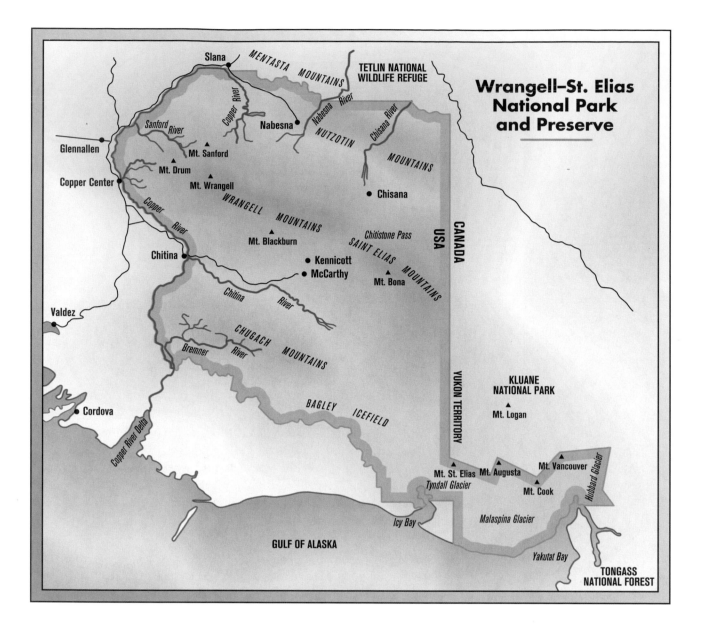

Wrangell–St. Elias
National Park
and Preserve

a full moon; and sphagnum moss that has never borne the imprint of a human boot. It is good to know there are such places.

Do not worry that you will have little to see. In a park the size of Wrangell-St. Elias, the area that *is* accessible is greater than most visitors will be able to explore. Two roads wind into the park area: the 60-mile (98-km) Chitina-McCarthy Road and the 42-mile (67-km) Nabesna Road. Several of the Wrangell volcanos—Mount Sanford, Mount Drum, and Mount Wrangell—are visible along the Alaska Highway from Tok to Glennallen and along the Richardson and Edgerton Highways. Mount Blackburn can be seen along the Chitina-McCarthy Road.

This is a place to scrutinize stones and note tree patterns. The tales of regional rocks, plants, animals, and humans are worthy of Scheherazade. Life here is raw, and survival is a celebration. Join in! Learn the stories and watch the land.

Fiery eruptions of lava are probably not the first images that come to mind as you gaze upon the icy mantles of Mounts Wrangell, Sanford, and Drum. But twenty-six million years ago—a short time in geological history—thick flows of molten rock formed the base of the Wrangell volcanos. Covering an area only a little smaller than the state of Connecticut, the Wrangells are evidence of the collision of land masses that created Alaska and the Yukon.

The park area comprises lands called *terranes* that rafted north on moving plates of the earth's crust over the last 300 million years. As each terrane collided

Tyndall Glacier

against the continent, pressure forced the leading edges to curve down into trenches on the ocean floor. These edges melted and eventually forced their way through fissures in the land to erupt as lava. Over time, lava flows formed volcanos. A simplified recipe for Baked Alaska, Wrangell-style.

The St. Elias and Chugach peaks also owe their presence to plate activity. As the Yakutat terrane pushes against the continent, lands crumple together like an automobile bumper in a fender-bender. Unlike your vehicle bumps, these crumplings create 18,000-foot (5,486-m) peaks. Please do not think of this as a piece of dusty history, for crumpling is occurring at this very moment: St. Elias peaks grow at least a quarter of an inch (about 0.5 cm) every year. The Bordercountry is anything but stagnant.

Glacier ice is both a remnant and an indication of things to come. The glaciers and icefields of the Wrangell-St. Elias area formed in the Ice Ages of the Pleistocene more than a million years ago and have advanced and retreated since. Icy Bay, located on the coast of the park, was filled with glacial ice just one hundred years ago. Glaciologists tell us that we are nearing the end of an ice-free period—in very brief geological time, much of the planet may again be as deep under ice as the Wrangell-St. Elias mountains.

Considering the high mountains, extreme temperatures, and icefields, the presence of life seems unlikely. Yet plants, animals, and humans have thrived in this seemingly inhospitable land for thousands of years.

One of the most fascinating things about the park is the opportunity to watch life take hold. Remember that Wisconsin, Ontario, New York, Alberta, Montana, and Nova Scotia also were under ice; some of these places looked similar to the Wrangells' town of McCarthy in the not-too-distant past.

Sit near the face of the Kennicott Glacier in McCarthy, and watch ice and rocks plummet into steel-blue meltwater. Over geological time, rocks surface and lichens take hold. Between the force of weather and lichen secretions, the rocks break down to gravel. Look at the spindly dryas plants rooting in the rocky soil. These hardy "pioneer" plants, the first leafy beings to settle the new land, contribute rich nitrogen to the ground. Turn around and see what the nitrogen-enriched soil brings: fireweed and cottonwood trees. Someday this area may be a coniferous forest. Someday this area may resemble Montana.

Where there are plants, there are animals. The berries, grasses, sedges, and mosses of the park brought herbivorous animals including moose, caribou, grouse, ground squirrels, marmots, and pika. With the herbivores came the carnivores and the omnivores: wolves, bear, lynx, coyote . . . and humans.

No one is sure when humans first inhabited the Bordercountry, but Native people have been in the area for several thousand years. In recorded time four distinct Native peoples have lived in the park area: Tlingits, Chugach Eskimo, Eyak, and Ahtna Athabaskans.

The Ahtna people occupied much of the interior park area. Climatic challenges required people to move seasonally with plants and animals. Summer fish camps were located near rivers with salmon runs, and permanent winter homes were closer to hunting and trapping grounds. Spring was the leanest time of year—when winter supplies of dried fish, game, and vegetation were low. Spring fishing often meant the difference between survival and starvation.

Under Wrangell-St. Elias ice, minerals cook in earth fires. Melted plate materials ooze up through fissures in surrounding rock and cool, forming large and small deposits. The Ahtna were the first to trade in the park area's rich mineral resources.

Little is known about trading before contact with the Russians and Americans, but early white explorers heard tales and saw trails that indicated an established copper trade between the interior Ahtna and the Tlingit of the coast. The Eyak may have been the go-betweens for the Ahtna and the Tlingit, trading copper for clams, seaweed, and other coastal goods.

Russians first reached the park area in 1741 with the voyage of Vitus Bering. A romantic legend recounts that fog surrounding Bering's ship lifted on the orthodox feast day of Saint Elias to reveal a towering triangle of ice, which Bering named after the Russian saint. Although the tale is probably untrue, the Icy Bay-St. Elias area was one of the Russians' first sightings of North America.

Furs, not gold, were the great lure of the area to the Russians. Russian fur traders came into the park region in the 1790s and established what they hoped would be a permanent trading post at Yakutat in 1795. Disputes between the Russians and the Yakutat Tlingits culminated in a battle in 1805 in which all the Russians were killed. The Russians did not try to reestablish the post.

Russians began exploring the interior Copper River region in the late 1790s. Because of the difficult climate and Russian-Athabaskan hostilities, the Russians had virtually abandoned the Copper Valley region by the 1850s.

Fall colors on the Nizine River

Rafting on the Copper River

The United States purchased "Seward's Folly" from Russia in 1867, and the United States Army began exploring the Copper River area in the 1880s. In 1884 Lieutenant Henry Allen began a remarkable 1,500-mile (2,414-km) journey into Alaska's interior, eventually traveling from the Copper River delta to the Koyukuk River via the Yukon River and the Tanana. Along the way he and his companions alternately starved and were feted in Ahtna villages, were aided and bamboozled by copper-wealthy Ahtna Chief Nicolai, drew the first maps of the region, (re)named the Wrangell volcanos, and visited Nicolai's copper lodes. Explorers and miners were still using Allen's maps to find their way to the Klondike twenty years later.

GOLD!! The glint of that four-letter word did more to lure humans to the Wrangell-St. Elias region than any number of fur-bearing creatures. Although the largest gold strikes were in the Yukon, thousands of hopeful gold diggers attempted to access the Klondike by way of Valdez, Copper Center, and the Mentasta Pass. The route was more difficult than most had anticipated. Many would-be millionaires either returned home or stayed to dig in the Wrangell and St. Elias Mountains.

Dan Kane was one of many miners who tried their luck in the craggy peaks of the St. Elias range. With monetary backing from one of the original funders of the Kennecott mining explorations, Kane started prospecting in an area across the Nizina River from McCarthy. Modestly christening the site of Chief Nicolai's copper source *Dan Creek*, Kane mined gold and copper beginning in 1901. Today the National Park Service maintains a station in the Dan Creek-May Creek area, and die-hard miners with gold dust in their eyes continue to dig the claims.

Those travelling the park's Nabesna Road are following the tracks of turn-of-the-century goldminers. Quartz gold was discovered at Jacksina Creek in 1899, but extraction difficulties limited production. Some claim a bear was responsible for the real gold find at Nabesna. The gopher-digging ursine apparently uncovered a vein promising enough to merit the founding of the Nabesna Mine. One of President Roosevelt's New Deal projects built the Nabesna Road in 1933, greatly aiding the mining process. Between 1931 and 1940 the mine produced and shipped over 70,000 tons (63,503 metric tons) of gold ore. Although the mine officially closed in the late 1940s, many—presumably including the present owners of the Nabesna Mine—still believe great gold riches lie below.

The last of the big-time gold rushes occurred in Chisana (pronounced Shuh-SHA-nuh), in the northeastern section of the park between the headwaters of the Chisana and White rivers. In 1913 news began to spread of a strike in the Chisana area. Commercial boosters from Dawson to Seattle were quick to promote anything that might resurrect the heady days of the Klondike stampede. Seattle businessmen who had watched in frustration as Klondike hopefuls purchased the majority of goods from Vancouver proprietors were more than ready to spread the word—regardless of truth—of this all-American bonanza. Not to be outdone, Canadian promoters moved quickly to advertise a Canadian route via Kluane Lake and the White River to Chisana.

Chisana today is mute testimonial to the power of a stampede. Once a town calling itself the largest log cabin community in the North, this remote site now is a town of log building ruins and home to but a hardy handful. A few miners hit paydirt, and a few shopkeepers and outfitters made a profit, but the majority of stampeders found starvation more likely than a strike. By 1916 the mining was all but finished, and most miners had turned homeward.

Overgrown trails and mining roads trace through the park from the infamous "Goat Trail" edging 1,000 sheer feet (300 m) above the Chitistone Canyon to the alder-filled Kotsina Road skirting Mount Blackburn. These mining leftovers are too remote for most park visitors, but know that cabins, stables, mine shacks, leather boot pieces, and iron tools litter park hills. Human impact is rarely as fleeting as human interest.

A grave site
near Kennecott Mine

For all the excitement over gold, the largest mineral find of the region was copper. The Kennecott Mines, located five miles (8 km) up a graded road from McCarthy, produced more than one billion pounds (nearly 500,000 kg) of copper between 1901 and the mine closure in 1938.

No doubt you shake your head in wonder as you walk between Kennecott mine buildings: How in the world did they build these behemoth structures way out in the middle of nowhere? Simple. Just mix money, motivation, and a deep faith in the right to dig anywhere one pleases. There were no federal laws requiring Environmental Impact Statements in those days. Financial support from some of America's most famous capitalists, J.P. Morgan and the Guggenheim brothers, did not hurt, either.

When one of the world's richest mineral deposits is discovered, remoteness is no obstacle. Between 1907 and 1911, as many as six thousand men worked summer and winter to build the Copper and Northwestern Railway between Cordova and Kennecott. They built a 1,500-foot (457-m) bridge strong enough to withstand the impact of glacier icebergs travelling downriver at 12 miles per hour (19 km/hour). They excavated five million cubic yards (nearly four million cubic meters) of rock and gravel. They laid track over 196 miles (315 km) and built 129 bridges. A few became wealthy. A few became even wealthier. Most accumulated a little money and a lot of good stories.

One thing the wealth-seekers had difficulty with was spelling. Intending to name the mine after explorer Robert Kennicott, someone misspelled the company's name as Kennecott. The nearby Kennicott glacier and river accurately reflect their namesake's surname.

Most of the people working at the Kennecott Mines were single men; many were immigrants with little command of English. Many young single women came to Kennecott as nurses and teachers and left as miners' wives. Children of supervisors and middle managers had fairytale years in the Hall of the Mountain King, skating, hiking, and drinking glacier-ice-cooled lemonade.

McCarthy was the town for fun and sin, offering everything from ice cream cones to saloons. Miners often spent all their hard-earned wages in a few McCarthy days, then headed uphill to start over again.

The Copper and Northwestern Railway operated until the mine closed in 1938 and then was dismantled for salvage during World War II. The gravel road you travel today between Chitina and McCarthy is, for the most part, the remains of the CR&NW Railway bed. Train cars loaded with copper steamed over that graded curve, and sweating muscles pounded steel down the gradual dip you now drive with ease toward the Chitina River.

Traveling the McCarthy Road today is an adventure, but be careful not to let the adventure become too interesting. Ghosts of Kennecott Past are wont to rise from the roadbed in the shape of iron-spiked railroad ties—take care to keep your eyes open and a spare tire in the trunk.

The lands and buildings of both McCarthy and Kennecott are presently in private ownership although the National Park Service is negotiating to acquire Kennecott. Please respect the rights of present owners and past spirits as you visit this rich area.

A lake along the McCarthy Road

Although few visitors will see the coastal portion of Wrangell-St. Elias, it is an extraordinary place. Home to threatened species (including the Steller sea lion, named after Russian scientist Georg Steller, and the marbled murrelet, a seabird), the Bordercountry coast is a place of new life. Much of the area is still under glacier ice. Forested lands are but a narrow corridor.

Coastal rainforest Sitka spruce sway on the edge of the Malaspina glaciers and harbor seals birth pups on icebergs floating in Icy Bay. Eagles nest, bears amble, Dungeness crab scurry. This delicate environment is protected only in part: Privately held lands on the south end of Icy Bay are threatened with logging. The era of Kennecott is not over.

McCarthy Lodge

Visiting the Park

The land status of Wrangell-St. Elias Park may be confusing to those not accustomed to Alaska. Wrangell-St. Elias is both a national park and a preserve. Sport hunting and trapping are allowed in the preserve, but only subsistence users (those who hunt and fish for personal food use) may hunt and trap in the park. Land holdings predating the 1980 establishment of the park and preserve, including recreational and mining sites, remain private property and are exempted from park regulations.

Most visitors—those who come to breathe in the magic of the Wrangells—will see no distinction between park and preserve. All are protected lands, facets of the ice-sculpted jewel we share with those who came before and those who come after. As you drive the Nabesna and McCarthy roads, hike the hills, climb the mountains, and ski the slopes, remember that this land is yours to enjoy and to protect. Rugged as they may appear, these peaks, streams, plants, and animals are vulnerable. They depend on you to pass through softly and to leave without trace of your visit.

In keeping with the wild spirit of the park, the National Park Service does not maintain the trails along the Nabesna and McCarthy roads or elsewhere in the park. This area is for you to discover and to travel as though you were the first. Some trails, including the Root Glacier trail from Kennecott, show signs of frequent use, at least for the first two miles. Others, including the path to Soda Lake from the Nabesna Road, may be difficult to trace.

Wrangell-St. Elias is wilderness in a world with little remaining wild country. Plan your park visit with a sense of discovery tempered by respect for remote and harsh country. There is something here for everyone, but know your limits. Weather can change quickly, and both black and brown bears roam throughout the park.

Approximately fifty miles (81 km) northwest of Yakutat, on the coast of the Gulf of Alaska, is a bay, barely a hundred years old, an infant in geologic time. Surrounded by the icy tentacles of Tyndall, Yahtse, and Guyot glaciers, Icy Bay appeared as the three glaciers retreated. This process continues today. The glaciers are part of the world's largest nonpolar ice field.

At the head of Icy Bay rises the 18,008-foot (5,485-m) Mount St. Elias. St. Elias is the third highest peak on the North American continent, and it climbs from sea level to summit within 15 miles (24 km). It is a beautiful peak, frequently hidden beneath clouds. Weather along the coast is usually inclement, with precipitation occurring as the moist Pacific air meets the mountains.

Our sea-kayaking trip began in light rain, overcast skies, and limited visibility; the usual weather for an area with over 130 inches (330 cem) of precipitation a year. Flying in from Yakutat, we landed on a flat section of beach just outside the Wrangell-St. Elias National Park boundary.

After assembling our kayaks, my three traveling companions and I spent our first afternoon exploring close to camp. An outgoing tide had carried icebergs and bergy bits away from the glacier face and into the bay. The ocean surrounding our beach had a slush-cup consistency. I felt as if I were afloat in a giant margarita. Taking turns playing icebreaker, we maneuvered the double kayaks toward the middle of the bay. Here we came across harbor seals, napping three or four to a berg. As we got closer, several seals surfaced near the kayaks, noses and eyes just breaking the ocean surface for a quick look before sinking back into the depths. We labeled them "spy seals."

As we paddled I was surprised to hear the hum of an approaching ship. Through the clouds and fog, a cruise ship loomed, sliding easily through the ice, heading for the glacier face. The appearance of the ship frac-

Paddling the Taan Fjord near 18,008-foot Mount St. Elias

tured the illusion of wilderness solitude, just as our arrival by airplane may have broken the spell for the one other party paddling in Icy Bay. This would not be the only boat traffic we would notice. That night the faint chug of a logging boat would be our goodnight lullaby.

Sunshine welcomed us the following morning. Breaking camp, we headed for Taan Fjord and the Tyndall Glacier. This glacier originates on Mount St. Elias and flows to tidewater at the mountain's base. The paddle along the steep, glacier-carved banks of the fjord was delightful. The mountain was mirrored in the calm waters. We seemed to be paddling up the mountain as the kayak bow sliced through granite outcropping and ice falls, creating an avalanche of ripples. Even the gulls appeared to be enjoying the day, swooping and diving in front of the glacier face, a 150-foot (46-m) wall of cracked and serrated bluish white ice.

Stretching our legs, we climbed the mountainside opposite the glacier. Here in rocks nearly 1000 feet (305 m) above sea level were marine fossils; a reminder that water levels change and the earth does not stand still. This realization was further reinforced that evening when we set up camp approximately eight miles (13 km) from the tidewater toe of the Tyndall Glacier. By examining an older map, we realized that our camp location had been under ice 10 years ago. Since that time the glacier had retreated over eight miles.

Huddled around a driftwood fire, we discussed Icy Bay and how fortunate we were to be experiencing

Tyndall Glacier ice

sunshine and clear skies. In the distance, Mount St. Elias's summit glowed faintly in the last light of day. Waters of the Taan Fjord were still, dark, and unfathomable, no longer mirroring the mountain. In the night sky, stars begin to appear, signaling the possibility of another clear day ahead.

What the Bordercountry Taught

I am in the City now.
        Computer screen letters glow
bright
        on black background:
C:\wp51\book\poem   Delete File? (No) Yes
Brown stains track lines down yellowed walls,
        pocked window panes frame splintered plywood fence.
            Sight is but one
vision.

In my mind's eye
        Harbor seals snort fish breath through wire whiskers
            Frost heaves
        From a brown bear snout
Air whistles in swan feather-flight
Ice rivers whisper blue, snaking
               serpentine gravel shadows
        White and black
        loons sing haunted arias across gray-green lakes
        Silver salmon splash
               sunlight pearls
        over cave-dark waters
               Snow crystals lace autumn
salmonberries
Fog soothes bony branches into lithe limbs.
               Continents collide, volcanos pour Pele's tears.

In my mind's mind
        I contact metamorphism;
            suspect terrane; and
        punctuate equilibrium.
I remark on
        ego/andro/euro/anthro   centric
        disdain
for the power

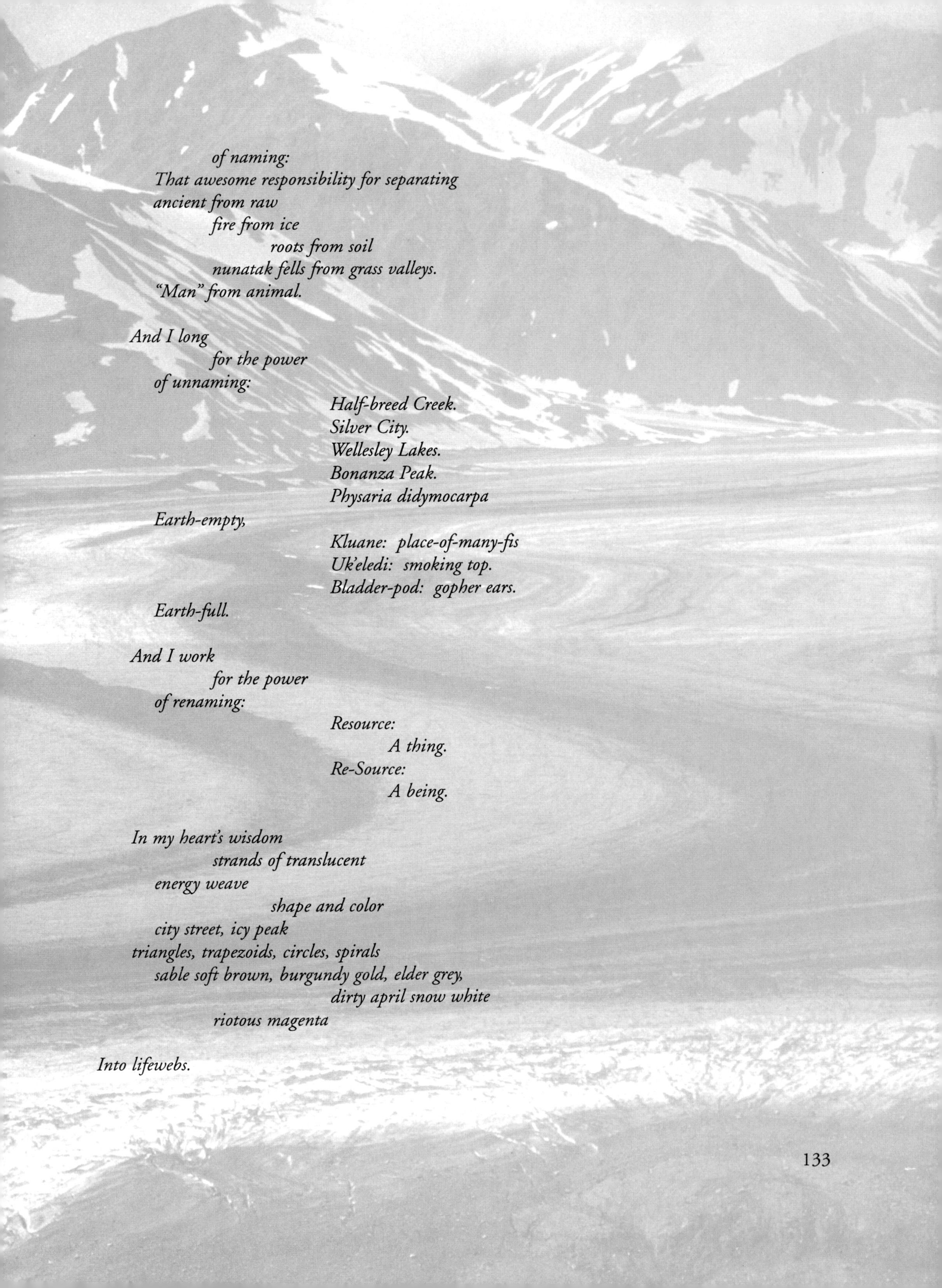

of naming:
That awesome responsibility for separating
ancient from raw
           fire from ice
                   roots from soil
               nunatak fells from grass valleys.
"Man" from animal.

And I long
           for the power
of unnaming:
                              Half-breed Creek.
                              Silver City.
                              Wellesley Lakes.
                              Bonanza Peak.
                              Physaria didymocarpa

       Earth-empty,
                              Kluane: place-of-many-fis
                              Uk'eledi: smoking top.
                              Bladder-pod: gopher ears.

       Earth-full.

And I work
           for the power
of renaming:
                              Resource:
                                       A thing.
                              Re-Source:
                                       A being.

In my heart's wisdom
           strands of translucent
       energy weave
                      shape and color
       city street, icy peak
triangles, trapezoids, circles, spirals
       sable soft brown, burgundy gold, elder grey,
                           dirty april snow white
           riotous magenta

Into lifewebs.

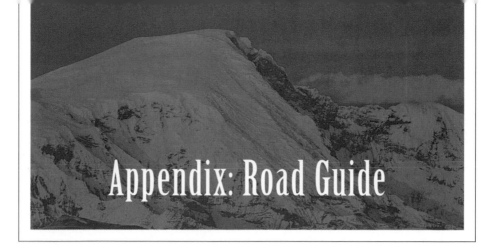

Appendix: Road Guide

Most visitors to Wrangell-St. Elias Park will travel either the Nabesna or McCarthy roads. Both of these roads are hazardous sometimes and breathless always. We hope this abbreviated road guide will aid in appreciating the human and natural history of this area. In keeping with our philosophy, we offer you information but leave the discoveries to you. Although we mention private businesses for your planning and safety, we endorse none of them. Safe journeys.

Nabesna Road to Glennallen

At Mile 59.8 (Km 96.2) of the Glenn Highway (Tok Cutoff), you can turn onto the 46-mile (74-km) Nabesna Road. The Park Service maintains a ranger station at Mile 0.2 (Km 0.3) in Slana, the small town along the first 2.5 miles (4 km) of Nabesna Road. Streams can make the Nabesna Road impassable, so check the ranger station for conditions. Do not forget to get a copy of the Park Service's brochure on the Nabesna Road.

The Nabesna Road runs southeast. As you drive in, the relatively gentle, low peaks on your left (northeast) are the Mentasta Mountains. These mountains are an extension of the Alaska Range, home to North America's highest peak, Denali (formerly Mount McKinley). To the south and southwest you see Capital Mountain (7,731 feet/2,356 m), Mount Jarvis (13,421 feet/4,091 m), and Tanada Peak (9,358 feet/2,853 m). The distinctive plateaulike slope rising to the south is Boomerang (3,949 feet/1,204 m). All are volcanos of the Wrangell Mountains and have not been active for at least one million years.

Nabesna Road

134

McCarthy Road

If the skies are clear you can see Mount Sanford (16,237 ft/4,949 m) jutting up behind Capital Mountain. Sanford is the second highest of the Wrangell volcanos and the thirteenth highest peak in North America. Sanford is a mountaineer skier's dream, offering thousands of vertical feet (or hundreds of meters) of glacier skiing. The south face of the peak is the steepest of the steeps, rising 8,000 feet (2,438 m) in one mile (1.61 km). Weather, however, often denies climbers the summit and roadside watchers a clear view. Your best chance of seeing Sanford is southeast of Slana on the Glenn Highway (Tok Cutoff) route to Gakona Junction and Glennallen.

There are no maintained campgrounds along the Nabesna Road, but camping is allowed at pullouts. Vista-rich tent sites abound next to lakes and on knolls just off the road. Several private lodges on the road offer rooms, meals, gas, air taxis, and guide services.

Grayling and burbot fishing is available at Long Lake, Mile 22.7 (Km 36.5). A lodge offers floatplane fishing trips to Copper and Tanada lakes. Each of these two large lakes is 200 feet (61 m) deep and contributes to the headwaters of the Copper River.

The unmaintained Twin Lakes campsites at Mile 28 (Km 45.1) are a quiet place to watch ducks paddle and to throw in a line for grayling, burbot, and lake trout. A lodge at Mile 28.5 (Km 45.9) offers guided fishing and hunting, rooms, meals, and gas.

Watch the Trail Creek crossing at Mile 29.4 (Km 47.3). At times this creek is impassable, and water levels may change during the day. The upper Trail Creek trail connects with the upper Lost Creek trail.

Lost Creek Trailhead at Mile 31.2 (Km 50.2) leads approximately eight miles (12.9 km) to the headwaters and is suitable for either a day hike or an overnight trip. Connect with the Trail Creek trail to loop back to the Nabesna Road.

Between Miles 32 and 42 (Km 52 and 68), the Nabesna Road follows a valley cutting through a portion of one of the oldest of the Wrangell mountains, the Skookum Creek volcano (7,125 ft/2,172 m). Looking to the southwest (to the right), you can see rock formations that were part of the two- to three-million-year-old volcano's flows. Skookum Creek volcano is the only mountain of the western Wrangells that is accessible from a road. A three-mile (nearly 5km) hike to the formations and side canyons will afford you an up-close-and-personal encounter with volcanic structures.

Jack Creek bridge crosses Mile 35.9 (Km 57.8). Look for unmaintained campsites in the area. At Mile 41 (Km 66) is Reeve's Field—an airstrip—and the trailhead of a five-mile (8-km) trail to the Nabesna River. A lodge offers guiding services at Mile 42 (Km 68).

State road maintenance ends at Mile 42 (Kmr 68). The final four miles (6 km) of the Nabesna Road lead to the Nabesna Mine and can be negotiated only with a four-wheel-drive vehicle. Owner permission is required to visit the privately owned mine. Look for white dots in the peaks on your left and right: The largest concentration of Dall sheep in Alaska resides in these craggy rocks.

Between Slana and Glennallen—if weather cooperates—you may have spectacular views of Mounts Sanford and Drum (12,010 ft/3,661 m). Lieutenant Henry Allen christened Sanford after a member of his family and Drum after a United States Army General. Although Mount Sanford is the taller of the peaks, Mount Drum is a demanding beauty looming large over the Copper River basin. If you should encounter these peaks on a clear Alaskan evening, you can watch the summer sun wash their icy mantles in golden pink.

Although you are not likely to see them, caribou utilize the area northwest of Sanford and Drum as a calving ground. In the fall, moose rut in the area.

Camping is available at the Alaskan State Dry Creek Recreation Site between Gulkana and Glennallen along the Glennallen Highway. The campgrounds are well kept, but you are sure to meet the most ominous animal of the North: the Bordercountry mosquito. Be forewarned.

On your way to McCarthy, stop at the Wrangell-St. Elias Park Headquarters at Mile 105 (Km 169) of the Old Richardson Highway. Watch for the turnoff sign south of Glennallen. The visitor center offers slide shows, books, tapes, and information on the park.

To reach Chitina, take the Edgerton Cutoff at Mile 35.1 (Km 56.5) of the Richardson Highway. Mounts Sanford, Drum, and Wrangell (14,163 ft/4,317 m) dominate the eastern horizon along the Richardson-Edgerton Highway. Mount Wrangell is the only known active volcano in the Wrangell Mountains. The Athabaskans knew Wrangell as Uk'eledi (Smoking Top) or K'elt'aene (The One That Controls). Lieutenant Henry Allen renamed the peak after Baron von Wrangell, a Russian Navy admiral and governor of Russian America from 1800 to 1836. Since the famous 1964 earthquake, the north crater of Mount Wrangell has billowed steam and fume clouds, early signs of a possible future eruption. The Richardson-Edgerton Highway also follows the Copper River and part of the trail leading to the Klondike gold fields.

From the Mentasta Pass on the Glenn Highway (Tok Cutoff) and down the Richardson-Edgerton Highway to Chitina, the road system passes through the Copper River basin. During the Pleistocene Ice Ages one million years ago, glaciers from surrounding mountain ranges covered the entire basin.

As glaciers blocked the Copper River, a huge lake formed, filling much of the basin. The lake, called Glacial Lake Ahtna, filled and drained with the advance and retreat of glaciers. Geologists believe the basin was water-filled as recently as 200,000 years ago. Ripples of Lake Ahtna sediments can be seen along the high bluffs above the Copper River.

Chitina to McCarthy

Chitina was established as a railroad town in 1908 during the construction of the Copper and Northwestern Railway. Chitina today is a sleepy town with a gas station-grocery store, post office, motel, and art gallery. The National Park Service maintains a ranger station in Chitina; be sure to check in for information and road conditions.

Between June and September, watch for Alaskans fishing for king and red salmon with dip nets in the Chitina River. You may also see fish wheels in operation. These ferris-wheel-like contraptions use paddles to scoop salmon from the water.

As you drive the road between Chitina and McCarthy, please be cautious and aware of other travellers, both human and nonhuman. Animals large and small use this road almost as much as humans. The road can become muddy and slippery after rains and may wash out after a heavy downpour. Be conscious of weather changes. Watch for spiked railway ties and carry a spare tire. Allow a minimum of three hours each way. Do not try to rush your visit; most people, however, spend at least two days exploring the McCarthy-Kennecott area.

The first part of the McCarthy Road cuts through a hardened mudslide that probably originated on the flanks of Mount Drum or Wrangell and slid almost forty-five miles (72 km) during an eruption at least 200,000 years ago. The slide materials are a mix of clay and volcanic rock.

The first bridge past Chitina, an expanse of 1,378 feet (420 m), takes you over the Copper River near its junction with the Chitina River. The Copper River drains most of the Wrangell region and is one of only two major rivers in the Alaska-Yukon region to drain into the Gulf of Alaska. Suspended glacial sediment from the Wrangell glacier colors the Copper and Chitina rivers an opaque gray. Water rushes through the Copper-Chitina Junction at 37,000 cubic feet (1,048 cu m) per second, one of the largest waterflows in North America.

The State of Alaska maintains an eight-site campground just on the other side of the Copper River bridge, with picnic tables, grills, and toilets. The confluence of the Copper and Chitina rivers brings frequent winds to the area, and the campground is not well sheltered. If you wear contact lenses, be careful of swirling glacial dust.

About 3.9 miles (6.3 km) down the road is a pullout with fine views of the Chitina River and the Chugach Mountains. The heavily glaciated Chugach Mountains span 300 miles (483 km) from the Anchorage area through Prince William Sound and grade into the St. Elias Mountains.

A pull-out at Mile 8.9 (Km 14.3) leads to Strelna Lake via a half-mile (.8-km) trail. The State of Alaska stocks several lakes in the area, including Strelna, Silver, and Sculpin lakes. Rainbow trout and silver salmon are ready for the catching, but respect the private property adjacent to the lakes. There are commercial campgrounds in this area.

At Mile 13.5 (Km 21.7) a track turning off to the left is the Kotsina Trail road. The backcountry trailheads for the Nugget Creek Trail, the Dixie Pass Trail, and the Kotsina Trail all start from points along this road. Ask at the Park Service offices for information on these hikes and for current conditions. Four-wheel drive is necessary, and do not plan on being able to drive more than the first 4 miles (6.4 km) of the road. Please respect the private property you pass on both sides of the Kotsina road.

The Nugget Creek Trail is approximately thirteen miles (21 km) from the crossing at Strelna Creek to the public use cabin on the far side of Nugget Creek.

A mountain bike is perfect for this trip, but expect to push it through muddy bogs for the first two miles (3 km). Streams can be fast, high, and very cold—crossings are not always possible. There is a nice halfway camp about seven miles (11 km) in for those who get a late start.

Autumn colors near Mount Sanford

Once you reach the Nugget Creek Cabin, you can hike along the Kuskulana Glacier or up side canyons and drainages. Mine ruins are located throughout the area. Please be cautious around old structures and stay out of mine tunnels.

If you are lucky, the view out your front door will be Mount Blackburn. When skies are clear, the glaciated giant appears close enough to touch. Some Blackburn climbers start from this location; you can read their stories in the visitor's log in the cabin.

You may choose to take a mountain bike trip for the full thirty-plus miles (51-plus km) of the Kotsina Road. The road is steep in parts and may be impassable due to high water, so remember the Scout credo and "Be Prepared." Mine ruins are common in this area, especially up the Elliot Creek drainage.

A third possibility is the hike over Dixie Pass, a three- or four-day backpacking trip on a 24-mile (38-km) loop. This hike will take you up game trails and over the 5,100-foot (1,555-m) pass.

If you skip the hikes and continue down the road, you will cross the Kuskulana River at Mile 17 (Km 27.4). Until 1988, the Kuskulana Bridge was one of the bigger thrills along the adventurous drive to McCarthy. Spanning the Kuskulana River (which drains a glacier of the same name at the foot of Mount Blackburn), the bridge is 238 feet (73 m) above the river and 525 feet (160 m) long. Imagine this bridge just one car length wide, with gaps between the wood decking and no guard rails: That was the Kuskulana bridge before its facelift in 1988. No longer able to raise their adrenaline just by crossing the bridge, thrill seekers have taken to illegally bungee-jumping into the canyon.

As the McCarthy Road passes over the Gilahina River at Mile 28.5 (Km 45.9), look at the railway trestle on your left. This was one of the 127 bridges of the Copper River and Northwestern Railway between Cordova and Kennecott.

Weather cooperating, you may catch some heart-stopping glimpses of Mount Blackburn to the north (on your left). Blackburn is the tallest of the Wrangell volcanos, stretching 16,390 feet (4,996 meters), and the twelfth highest mountain in North America. Some of its volcanic rocks are more than 4 million years old, but most of the Blackburn granite is approximately 3.5 million years old. The massif is

Mount Blackburn

almost completely ice covered. The Kennicott Glacier near McCarthy and Kennicott flows from Blackburn. Mount Blackburn ice also contributes to the waters of the Nabesna River on the north side of the park/preserve.

A turnout at Mile 57.3 (Km 92.2) on the right side of the road affords an overlook view of McCarthy and the toe of the Kennicott Glacier. You have almost reached the road terminus.

McCarthy and Kennecott

McCarthy is not accessible by road and requires a trip across the Kennicott River in a hand-pulled tram. Do not cross on the trams unless you and members of your party are capable of pulling the cable gondolas across several hundred feet (a hundred meters or so).

The most efficient way to pull the trams is through cooperation with whoever may be on the other side: You help pull them and they do the same for you. The

McCarthy tram is an example of the way strangers can become friends. Pack work gloves to use in pulling the cables—you will be glad you have them. If you cannot operate the trams, use the radio telephone at the first tram to locate assistance.

Once across the Kennicott River, McCarthy is a short walk away. As you meander along the road you will pass a clear stream on your left. This stream is the water source for local residents, so please help keep it clean. The buildings in McCarthy are privately owned; respect them as you would anyone's home.

The local museum, located in the old train depot, has exhibits of historical artifacts and photographs from McCarthy's heydays. At the time of this writing, McCarthy has two lodges, a restaurant and bar, and guiding and flight-seeing services. None of these businesses are connected with the park service.

A bus offers rides to the Kennecott Mine, or you may walk or bike the four miles (6 km) up the gently graded road. Once at Kennecott, you will see the recently expanded Kennicott Glacier Lodge and Restaurant on your right. The lodge also offers historical walks through Kennecott.

The buildings of Kennecott are privately owned and potentially dangerous: Please do not enter them. You are free to peek in the windows and wander the area. You will see the power plant, the mill and leaching plant, the supply store, the infirmary, the staff house, and several individual homes.

As you look beyond the buildings to the left, you may feel shocked to see what appear to be piles and piles of mining tailings stretching as far as the eye can see. Human hands were not involved in these landscape changes. Those gray rocks are actually part of the Kennicott Glacier and cover the ice underneath. Someday trees will grow from that seemingly barren rockfield.

Hiking in the McCarthy Area

We remind you again that the philosophy of the Wrangell-St. Elias Park is one of light steps and self-discovery. Although there are numerous trails through the park, they long predate the Park Service and are not maintained today. You will find no mileage markers or information booths. You may find bears. And if you approach a glacier, you will understand why we refer to glaciers as "flowing": Large ice and rock pieces often fall; creaking crevasses yawn wide and deep. For the most part, you are on your own here. Please respect this country and your own limits.

One of the most popular hikes in the area is to follow the road through Kennecott as it turns into the Root Glacier Trail. The trail crosses several streams in the first three miles (nearly 5 km), including Bonanza, Jumbo, and National

Nabesna Mine

creeks. As you hike, you may notice you are walking the ridge of a lateral moraine: Eventually the trail becomes but a narrow edge. The trail dips down to the glacier and continues on to the Stairway Icefall; go as far as you desire and return the same way you came. Bears frequent this area and alder is thick. Make noise and stay alert for bear activity.

Few hikers venture beyond the Stairway Glacier to Bonanza Ridge, McCarthy Creek, and back to McCarthy. Travelers who do, will see a *jokulhlaup* (a glacier-dammed lake), waterfalls, close views of the Stairway Icefall, and Mount Blackburn. The MotherLode Mine is visible on this route, and a side trip will take trekkers to Nikolai Pass and views of the Chitistone Gorge. These multiday trips are for experienced hikers only, and cross private property.

Another possibility is to access the Root Glacier just beyond Jumbo Creek, cross the Root Glacier, and hike to Donoho Peak, the green mountain in the middle of the Kennicott and Root glaciers. This 14-mile (nearly 23-km) hike offers unique views of Kennecott and the glaciers but is for experienced hikers and glacier travelers only.

A day hike to the Bonanza Mine is possible from the Kennecott Mine road. The road turns to the right off the path to the Root Glacier and climbs to the Bonanza Mine site at 5,950 feet (1,814 m). The climb is a workout but is not technically difficult. From the top hikers can see ruins of the Bonanza Mine, the entrance to the mine tunnel, and a circular expanse of glaciers, rivers, and greenery. Please stay away from the tunnel—it is unsafe.

Visitors also may walk to the face of the Kennicott Glacier. Just follow the road through McCarthy past the General Store and cross a creek on a small footbridge. You will find yourself at the bud of creation. Watch rocks fall into glacier meltwater, and trace the mat of dryas flowers rooting rock to soil. This is how life begins.

Experienced hikers may want to explore routes in the May Creek area or through the spectacular Chitistone Gorge. These trips will require airplane time because the Nizina River cannot be crossed.

The Nabesna area

For those without a fear of heights, the Chitistone Gorge is a small Yosemite, complete with a 300-foot (91-meter) waterfall and wind-sculpted limestone spires. The catch is the Goat Trail, a white-knuckle scree trail edging along drops of several thousand feet (a hundred meters or so) and glacier river crossings that are impassable at times. But if your timing is right and you do not mind looking at clouds between your feet, the Chitistone Gorge is one of the great sights of North America.

Whether you come to Wrangell-St. Elias National Park and Preserve for a long weekend or for long weeks, you are sure to leave with memories for a lifetime. This place is part of your home and the home of your children's children. Enjoy your visit and walk softly through one of the world's last great wilderness areas.

Suggested Reading List

Alaska-Yukon Wildflowers Guide. Anchorage: Alaska Northwest Books: 1979.

Allen, Lt. Henry Allen, *An Expedition to the Copper, Tanana, and Koyukuk Rivers in 1885.* Anchorage: Alaska Northwest: 1985.

Armstrong, Robert. *Guide to the Birds of Alaska.* Anchorage: Alaska Northwest Books: 1990.

Bodeau, Jean. *Katmai National Park and Preserve, Alaska.* Anchorage: ANHA and Greatland Graphics: 1992.

Champagne-Aishihik Indian Band and Sha-Tan Tours, *From Trail to Highway.* Victoria, B.C.: 1988.

Connor, Cathy and O'Hare, William. *Roadside Geology of Alaska.* Missoula: Mountain Press Publishing Co.: 1988.

Cruikshank, Julie. *Life Lived Like a Story.* Lincoln: University of Nebraska Press: 1990.

Davis, Neil. *Alaska Science Nuggets.* Anchorage: University of Alaska: 1989.

Fitzhugh, William and Aron, Crowell. *Crossroads of Continents: Cultures of Siberia and Alaska.* Washington D.C.: Smithsonian Institute Press: 1988.

Fuller, Margaret. *Mountains.* New York: John Wiley & Sons, Inc.: 1989.

Hampton, Bruce and Cole, David. *Soft Paths.* Harrisburg: Stackpole Books: 1988.

Hunt, William R. *Mountain Wilderness.* Washington D.C.: National Park Service: 1991.

Irwin, Stephen. *Hunters of the Northern Forest.*

Langdon, Steve. *The Native People of Alaska.* Anchorage: Greatland Graphics: 1987.

Larson, Richard. *Mountainbiking in Alaska.* 1992.

Lopez, Barry. *Arctic Dreams.* New York: Charles Scribner & Sons: 1986.

McClellan, Catherine. *Part of the Land, Part of the Water.* Vancouver, B.C.: Douglas & McIntyre: 1978.

McPhee, John. *Assembling California.* 1993.

National Park Service. *Access National Parks: A Guide for Handicapped Visitors.* Washington D.C.: 1978.

Nelson, Richard. *Make Prayers to the Raven.*

O'Clair, Rita, Armstrong, Robert and Cartensen, Richard. *The Nature of Southeast Alaska.* Anchorage: Alaska Northwest: 1992.

Pratt, Verna. *Field Guide to Alaskan Wildflowers.* Anchorage: Alaskakrafts Publishing: 1989.

Rearden, J. *Mammals of Alaska*: Alaska Geographic 8 (2). Anchorage: Alaska Northwest Books: 1981.

Schofield, Janice. *Alaska's Wild Plants.* Anchorage: Alaska Northwest Books: 1993.

Starhawk. *The Fifth Sacred Thing.* 1994.

Thebarge, John, ed. *Kluane: Pinnacle of the Yukon.* 1974.

Williams, Terry Tempest. *Refuge: An Unnatural History.* 1992.

Zimmerman, Jenny. *A Naturalist's Guide to Chugach State Park, Alaska.* Anchorage: A.T. Publishing and Printing, Inc.: 1993.